Rod and Staff Books

(Milestone Ministries)

800-761-0234 or 541-466-3231

www.RodandStaffBooks.com

THE **Building Christian English** SERIES

Building

Christian English

Preparing to Build

Grade 2

Rod and Staff Publishers, Inc.
Crockett, Kentucky 41413

Telephone (606) 522 4348

Acknowledgments

Repeatedly God has commanded men to write. Today the Gospel must be shared. The urgency of this has prompted the publication of this text. Rachel Christopher wrote the text. Lester Miller and Susie Hoover did the illustrating. Anna Mary Kauffman, Rose (Gingrich) Biehn, and Paul and Mary Landis gave helpful reviews. Others have worked many hours to make the text available. We pray the Kingdom of God will benefit from these efforts.

We wish to express our appreciation to the *Mennonite Publishing House,* Scottdale, Pa. for use of the poems "Love," and "A Smile, A Word" from *Poems for Our Boys and Girls,* no. 2, edited by Lina Ressler.

Copyright, 1983
By
Rod and Staff Publishers, Inc.
Crockett, Kentucky 41413
Printed in U.S.A.

ISBN 0-7399-0508-2
Catalog no. 12202.3

16   17   18   19   —   15   14   13   12   11   10   09   08   07

Table of Contents

The Gift of Language

God made people in a special way. He gave us certain special gifts which He did not give to the animals and plants. God gave us a soul and a spirit. He also gave us a mind with which to think.

Language is another special gift from God. God gave us language to use to communicate with one another. When we want to tell someone else what we are thinking, we usually use language. When we read or write, we use the gift of language.

God also gave us language so that He can communicate with us. The Bible is one way in which God uses language to communicate with us. When we read the Bible, we are reading what God wants us to know.

When God first made people, He gave them only one language. All the people could understand each other. Many years later, God confused their language. He gave different people different languages.

Now there are many languages in the world. The language that we speak is called English. Most of the people in the United States of America and in Canada speak English.

This year, as you study language, you will be studying English. You will be learning many things about the way we speak and write in the English language. You will learn different ways to use the English language to share with others what you are thinking.

Who made the world?

God made the world.

Unit 1

Learning About Sentences

"I will meditate also of all thy work, and talk of thy doings."

Psalm 77:12

1. What Is a Sentence?

God made the sentence. He built it with words. The following group of words is a sentence. It is a lovely thought about God.

God is love.

We did not always think and speak in sentences. First we thought or said only one word at a time. If we were thirsty, we thought, "Drink." So we did not say to Mother, "Please give me a drink." We only said, "Drink."

After a while we learned to think and say two or more words together. We may have said, "Drink good." This still was not a sentence. It did not make a complete thought.

Finally, we learned to think and speak in sentences. Now we would not say, "Drink good." We would say, "This drink is good." This is a complete thought. It is a sentence.

A sentence is a complete thought.

> **For You to Do**

Copy each sentence below. Choose the correct word to finish each sentence.

complete   sentence   words

1. God made the ——.
2. He built it with ——.
3. A sentence is a —— thought.

Finding Sentences

After each number below there are two groups of words. One group of words is a sentence. The other group of words is not a sentence. On your paper, write **a** or **b** after each number to tell which group of words is a sentence.

1. a. Loves me.
   b. God loves me.

2. a. God is kind.
   b. Is kind.

3. a. God very good.
   b. God is good.

4. a. Is very wise.
   b. God is wise.

5. a. He cares for us.
   b. Cares for us.

6. a. Loves God.
   b. We love God.

7. a. Jesus loves us.
   b. Loves us.

8. a. We to Him.
   b. We pray to Him.

9. a. We thank Him.
   b. We Him Thanks.

10. a. He hears us.
    b. Hears us.

Writing Sentences

Find the sentences below. Copy them onto your paper.

1. Cannot see God.
2. God sees us all the time.
3. He gives us all we need.
4. Food and clothes.
5. He makes everything grow.
6. He fresh air.
7. He is a wonderful God.

2. Phrases

We learned that a group of words which has a complete thought is called a sentence. Some groups of words do not have a complete thought.

Groups of words that do not have a complete thought are called phrases.

Sometimes when we talk we use phrases. Read the following conversation.

"Where are your books?" Sister Anne asked.

"In my desk," John answered.

"My books are in my desk," Carl added.

"In my desk" is not a complete thought. It is a phrase. "My books are in my desk," is a complete thought. This group of words is a sentence.

God wrote the Bible with complete thoughts. God wrote the Bible with sentences. When we write, we should use sentences also.

> For You to Do >

Read each group of words below. Write **S** after the number on your paper if the group of words is a sentence. Write **P** if the group of words is a phrase.

1. I will sing.
2. In a basket.
3. Jesus wept.
4. Daniel prayed.
5. Mary and Martha.
6. God's only Son.
7. We love God.
8. Kind and good.
9. God is good.
10. Always praying.

More Practice and Review

After each number below there are two groups of words. Copy the group of words in each set that is a sentence.

1. Obeyed God.
   Noah obeyed God.
2. He built an ark.
   Built an ark.
3. Noah went into the ark.
   Noah in the ark.
4. Made it rain.
   Then God made the rain fall.
5. Noah and his family were safe.
   Noah and his family.
6. Thanked God.
   They thanked God.

Read the sentences you copied. Do they make a story? Now read the phrases you did not copy. Do they make a story?

3. The *Telling* Sentence

We use sentences to tell what we know. Do you know who made the birds?

God made the birds.

This sentence tells us that God made the birds. It is a telling sentence. Read these sentences.

God is holy.   God loves us.

These sentences tell us about God. They are telling sentences. The Bible tells us many things about God. The Bible has many telling sentences. We read the Bible to learn more about God.

Look at the sentences about God. Do you see the mark at the end of each sentence? This mark (.) is a **period**. The **period** shows us where each telling sentence ends. Read these sentences.

God made the flowers Birds sing

Do you know where each sentence ends? Now read these sentences.

God made the flowers.   Birds sing.

We use the period to show where a telling sentence ends.

A sentence that tells ends with a period.

$\rhd$ **For You to Do** $\rhd$

Find the first verse in your Bible. Copy this verse onto your paper. Be ready to say what the verse tells about God.

> **More Practice and Review** >

A. After each number below there are two groups of words. Copy the group of words that is a sentence. Be sure to end each sentence with a period.

1. Peter caught
   Peter caught fish

2. Jesus called Peter
   Called Peter

3. Peter left his nets
   Peter his nets

4. Followed Jesus
   He followed Jesus

5. Andrew too
   Andrew followed Jesus, too

B. After each number is a group of words. Each group of words is two sentences. Copy the sentences properly. End each sentence with a period (.).

1. Some animals eat roots They are rodents

2. Beavers eat roots Beavers are rodents

3. God gave them sharp teeth They can bite hard roots

4. God made many other rodents He is a great God

4. The *Asking* Sentence

God made sentences for us to use. He made sentences that we can use to tell what we know. Sentences that tell are called **telling** sentences. God also made sentences that we can use to ask. **Asking** sentences are called **questions**. Read this sentence.

Who was Isaac's mother?

This sentence does not tell. It **asks** us who Isaac's mother was. This sentence is a **question**. Read the following sentence.

Sarah was Isaac's mother.

This sentence tells us who Isaac's mother was. This sentence is a telling sentence. It answers our question. We found this answer in the Bible. We find answers to many questions in the Bible.

Look at the asking sentence. Does it end with a period? No, asking sentences end with a special mark. This mark (?) is called a **question mark**.

A sentence that asks ends with a question mark.

> For You to Do

Copy these asking sentences. End each one with a question mark. Next to each question write its answer. Use the Bible to help you.

1. What must children do (Ephesians 6:1)
2. Where did Jesus see Nathaniel (John 1:48)

3. Who wrote the Book of Revelation (Revelation 1:4)

> More Practice and Review >

Read the sentences below. Some of the sentences tell. Some of the sentences ask. On your paper, write **tells** if the sentence tells. Write **asks** if the sentence asks something.

1. Who was Samuel's mother?
2. Hannah was Samuel's mother.
3. She gave Samuel to the Lord.
4. Do you know where Samuel lived?
5. He lived with Eli.
6. Eli was the high priest.
7. Who called Samuel?
8. Who spoke to Samuel?
9. God called Samuel.
10. Samuel obeyed God.

5. Reviewing What We Have Learned

A. On your paper write the correct word to complete each sentence below.

> complete   period   God   tells
> words   phrase   asks   question mark

1. —— made the sentence.
2. He built it with ——.
3. A sentence is a —— thought.
4. A —— is not a complete thought.
5. The telling sentence ——.
6. The asking sentence ——.
7. The telling sentence ends with a ——.
8. The asking sentence ends with a ——.

> Remember: God gave us the sentence. He gave us the sentence to use. We should use good sentences. We should use sentences that please God.

B. Copy the sentences that please God.

1. I will help you, Mother.
2. I do not want to work.
3. We sing about Jesus.
4. Don't touch my books.
5. You may read my new book.

C. Read the groups of words below. Five of them are telling sentences. Five of them are asking sentences. Five of them are phrases. Copy the groups of words that are sentences. End each sentence with the proper mark.

1. Who saw Jesus
2. Peter saw Jesus
3. On the shore
4. Jesus was on the shore
5. In the boat
6. Who was in the boat
7. The men were in the boat
8. Were frightened
9. They were frightened
10. Who walked on the water
11. Who stopped the storm
12. On the water
13. Who helped them
14. Jesus helped them
15. Came and helped

6. Starting Sentences Correctly

God made man in a good way. He made man able to speak and to write. God gave man the right to make rules. He gave man the wisdom to make helpful rules. Man has made many rules to help us know how to write correct sentences. Here are two rules we learned.

A sentence that tells ends with a period.
A sentence that asks ends with a question mark.

These rules help us know where a sentence ends. We also have a rule to help us know where a sentence begins. This is the rule:

Every sentence begins with a capital letter.

Every sentence we write should begin with a capital letter. Look at the sentences on this page. They each begin with a capital letter. We must remember to use a capital letter to begin every sentence we write.

These are the twenty-six letters of the alphabet. Each of them has a capital letter and a small letter. Learn how to write the capital letters neatly and correctly.

Aa Bb Cc Dd Ee Ff Gg Hh Ii
Jj Kk Ll Mm Nn Oo Pp Qq Rr
Ss Tt Uu Vv Ww Xx Yy Zz

For You to Do

A. Write the twenty-six capital letters on your paper. Remember to use these letters to begin sentences.

B. Study the three rules that you learned about sentences. Close your book and write these rules from memory. Open your book and check your work. Did you write them correctly?

More Practice and Review

Below are ten sentences. They do not begin properly. Write correctly the first word of each sentence. Begin each word with a capital letter.

1. god made everything.
2. first He made the light.
3. he also made the earth and sky.
4. on the third day God made plants.
5. next He made the sun, moon, and stars.
6. do you know what God made then?
7. then God made the birds and fish.
8. when did God make the animals?
9. finally God made man.
10. then God rested.

7. Beginning and Ending Sentences

We learned that we use capital letters to begin sentences. We can use periods and question marks to end sentences. We use these as signs when we build sentences.

People who build roads use signs, too. Traffic lights are signs. These signs tell people when to **go** and when to **stop**. A green light means **go**. A red light means **stop**. These signs help people drive carefully.

Our sentence signs help us read carefully. A capital letter tells us to begin reading. A period or question mark tells us to stop reading. Read these sentences:

 I like fall the leaves change color some are orange and red others are yellow God made fall beautiful

These sentences do not have any signs to tell us where each sentence begins and ends. We do not know when to begin reading and when to stop. Now read the sentences below.

I like fall. The leaves change color. Some are orange and red. Others are yellow. God made fall beautiful.

These sentences are easier to read. They are written properly. The sentence signs tell us when to begin and when to stop.

> For You to Do

Practice reading the sentences about fall. Make

your voice "stop" at the period. Make your voice "go" at the capital letter.

> Using What You Have Learned >

A. Copy these telling sentences. Begin each one with a capital letter. End each one with a period.

1. the Bible is perfect
2. it is God's Word
3. we love this good Book
4. it has many wonderful stories
5. the stories teach us about God

B. Copy these asking sentences. Begin each one with a capital letter. End each one with a question mark.

1. who came to the tomb
2. where was Jesus
3. what did the angel say
4. how many people saw Jesus
5. did Peter see Jesus

8. Making Sentences

We use words to make sentences. God gave us words. He gave us words to help put pictures in our minds. Read these words:

girl   bird   dog

These words bring pictures to our minds. We can see a girl, a bird, and a dog. What is the girl doing? What are the bird and the dog doing? Read these phrases:

bakes a cake   sings a song   runs quickly

Can you picture the girl baking a cake? Can you picture the bird singing and the dog running? When we put words together we add more details to the pictures in our minds.

The girl bakes a cake.

These words are a complete thought. These words make a complete sentence. Each word helps carry a picture to our minds. We see a girl. We know she is baking. We know she is baking a cake.

> **For You to Do** >

A. Choose the best phrase to complete each sentence. Write the phrase after the correct number on your paper.

1. The wind ——.   **go to school**

2. This orange ——.   **is blowing**

3. We ——.   **loves us**

4. Jesus ——.   **are baking bread**

5. Ruth and Mother ——.   **is juicy**

B. Choose the best word or phrase to begin each sentence. Write the word or phrase after the correct number on your paper.

1. —— are singing.   **The leaves**

2. —— is at the door?   **Sarah**

3. —— are green.   **Many children**

4. —— gave us the Bible.   **Who**

5. —— cooks supper.   **God**

> **More Practice and Review** >

Read the sentences below. They do not begin and end properly. Copy them correctly on your paper.

where is God he is in heaven he sees
all that we do God never sleeps he takes
care of us we thank God for His care

9. Making More Sentences

The Bible is God's Word. We know that every sentence in the Bible is true. "Thy word is truth," (John 17:17) is a sentence in the Bible. This sentence reminds us that every word God speaks is the truth.

God wants our words to be true, too. We should never say anything that is not true. The sentences that we write must also be true and right. Whether we speak or write, we must always use words that tell the truth.

Our sentences should always please God. We should not say or write anything that is unkind or foolish. God is not pleased with unkind or foolish words. Read these sentences.

> **Noah crossed the Red Sea.**
> **That girl looks funny.**
> **Jesus wants us to help others.**

Which sentence pleases God? The first sentence is not true. The second sentence is not kind. The third sentence is a good thought. These words are true and kind. They are not foolish. Only the third sentence would please God.

Words we speak, and words we write, Must be true and must be right.

▷ For You to Do ▷

Choose the best word or phrase to complete each

sentence. Write the sentences on your paper.

1. We should ——.   **tease kittens**
                       help others

2. John ——.   **is a good brother**
                       always cries

3. Let me ——.   **do what I want to do**
                       help you

4. School is ——.   **God's gift to us**
                       too much work

> **More Practice and Review**

Choose the best word or phrase to complete each sentence. Write the sentences correctly, using capital letters and end marks.

1. many people ——   **the people**
2. —— built a tower   **what God did**
3. god ——   **god**
4. do you know ——   **lived together**
5. —— changed their language   **was not pleased**

10. Reviewing What We Have Learned

A. Write from memory the three rules you have learned about the beginnings and endings of sentences. Turn to lesson 6 to check your work.

B. On your paper write the correct word to complete each sentence below.

> thought   unkind   minds   sentences
> every   true   God

1. God's Word is ——.
2. Our sentences should please ——.
3. God is not pleased with —— words.
4. Words make pictures in our ——.
5. We use words to make ——.
6. A sentence is a complete ——.
7. —— sentence starts with a capital letter.

C. Next to each sentence below is a picture. Use the picture to find a word or phrase to complete each sentence. Write the complete sentence on your paper.

1. The boys ——.

2. Mary ——.

3. —— slept.

4. —— put the toys away.

5. —— are pretty.

D. Some of the groups of words below are sentences. Some of them are phrases. Copy correctly the sentences that please God. Remember to follow the rules.

1. jesus is our friend
2. get out of my way
3. rain and snow
4. would you please help me
5. have to help
6. we will dry the dishes
7. why should I work
8. my sister is kind

11. Building More Sentences

Did you ever build a birdhouse? First you had to find a piece of wood to be the floor. Then you chose other pieces of wood to be the sides and roof. If you were building the house for a wren, you used small pieces of wood. If you were building the house for a dove, you used bigger pieces of wood.

When we build sentences, we have to choose our words. First we choose a word that says who or what the sentence is about. If we want to talk about a **dog**, we do not choose the word **flower**. We choose the word **dog**, or **pup**, or **puppy**.

Puppy is not a sentence. We must choose more words to help build our sentence. We ask ourselves, "What did the puppy do?"

Choose one of these words to say what the puppy did.

sewed   read   barked   fished

We would choose the word **barked**. Now we know what the puppy did. Now we know what words to use to build our sentence.

The puppy barked.

This is a good sentence. The words make sense and are not foolish. We want all our sentences to be sensible. We want them to be true and kind. Then our sentences will please God.

For You to Do

Write five sentences. Choose a word from **column A** to tell who or what the sentence is about. Choose a word from **column B** to tell what happened. Use each word only once. Remember to begin and end every sentence correctly. Read your sentences to be certain they are sensible.

A	B
fish	fell
leaves	mewed
children	shone
what	swam
stars	sang

More Practice and Review

A. Below are five words. Each word tells what happened. On your paper write who or what did each word below.

1. baked
2. hammered
3. galloped
4. rang
5. flew

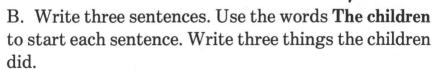

B. Write three sentences. Use the words **The children** to start each sentence. Write three things the children did.

12. Writing What We Know

Did anybody ever ask you your name? What did you answer? Did you say Susan? or John? or Paul? You said your own name.

If you said only your name, you did not say a sentence. When we speak we do not always need to use sentences. When we write we must write complete thoughts. We must write complete sentences. Read these words:

Paul   Hope   eight

Do you understand what these words mean? Now read the words below.

> My name is **Paul**.
> I go to **Hope** Christian Day School.
> I am **eight** years old.

These are complete sentences. We can understand what these sentences mean.

> Remember: When we write we should use complete sentences. We should write clearly so that people can understand what our words mean. We should choose good answers and write what is true and correct.

> For You to Do >

Copy the sentences below. Use a correct word (or words) to complete each sentence.

1. My name is ——.
2. I go to —— Christian Day School.
3. I am —— years old.
4. I am in the —— grade.
5. Today's date is ——.

> More Practice and Review >

Choose the best word or phrase to complete each sentence. Remember to begin each sentence with a capital letter. Remember to end each sentence with the correct mark.

1. mother ——.	**the children**
2. the house ——.	**Mother**
3. —— loved Mother	**was tired**
4. they ——.	**was cluttered**
5. —— thanked the children	**put the toys away**

Read your sentences. Do they make sense? Do they make a story?

13. Writing More Sentences

God made many good things. We thank Him for the wonderful things He has made. Can you name something God has made?

God made ——.

What word did you use to complete the sentence above? Did you say birds? or fish? or stars? We could choose many words to complete this sentence. The sentence would still be true. Read these sentences.

God made light.
God made water.
God made clouds.

God gave us many words. When we write, we can use the many different words God gave us. We do not need to always write the same thing. Read this sentence. Use different words to complete the sentence.

God is ——.

It is easy to think of one word. It is easy to think of two or three words.

God is holy.
God is great.
God is good.

How many more words can you think of to complete this sentence?

God gave us our minds. He wants us to use our minds to think. He wants us to think good thoughts.

It is not always easy to think. Sometimes we must make our minds work hard. God wants us to work with our hands and with our minds, too. We must work with our minds if we are to build good sentences.

> For You to Do >

Write these sentences. Choose a good word to complete each sentence.

1. I have a ——.
2. The grass is ——.
3. —— loves me.
4. Mother makes ——.
5. Paul read a ——.

> More Practice and Review >

Copy each sentence below, but do not copy the word in bold print. Choose a word from the list to complete each sentence. Write this word where the word in bold print was.

1. The flowers are **pretty**.   letter
2. Please pass the **bread**.   ate
3. Samuel **obeyed** God.   butter
4. Mother read a **book**.   yellow
5. Who **made** supper?   praised

14. Answering Questions

We learned about two kinds of sentences. We learned that some sentences **tell** what we know. These are telling sentences. We learned that some sentences **ask**. We call sentences that ask **questions**. Read this question:

Who was David's father?

Do you know the answer to this question? Read the word below. Is it the correct answer?

Jesse

Jesse is the correct answer to the question. But **Jesse** is not a complete thought. It is not a sentence. Now read these words:

David's father was Jesse.

This is a complete sentence. This sentence answers our question. It tells us who David's father was. It is a telling sentence.

When we answer questions, we should use complete sentences. We should use sentences that tell the answer.

> Remember: to answer questions we use telling sentences.

For You to Do

Next to each number below are two sentences. The first sentence is a question. The second sentence is not complete. Write the words of the second sentence on your paper. Then choose a good word to answer the question. Use this word to complete the sentence on your paper.

1. Who is your teacher?
   My teacher is ——.
2. Where was Moses born?
   Moses was born in ——.
3. Where is Jesus?
   Jesus is in ——.
4. What do we write?
   We write ——.
5. What did God write?
   God wrote the ——.

More Practice and Review

Read the sentences below. Copy the sentences but do not copy the underlined word. Make your mind think. Think of another word to complete the sentence. Write this word instead of the underlined word.

1. I like to <u>sing</u>.   3. The horse <u>trotted</u>.
2. God made <u>me</u>.   4. A <u>cow</u> is outside.

15. Reviewing What We Have Learned

A. Write five sentences. Use a word or phrase from **column A** to begin your sentence. Use a word or phrase from **column B** to complete your sentence.

<u>A</u>	<u>B</u>
the people	is warm
everybody	blew
the wind	was singing
the weather	flew
what	were praying

B. Choose a good word to complete these sentences. Write the sentences on your paper.

1. I have —— eyes.

2. I have two ——.

3. My hair is ——.

4. I —— with my ears.

5. —— made me in a good way.

Whatsoever things are true,
Whatsoever things are honest,
Whatsoever things are just,
Whatsoever things are pure,
Whatsoever things are lovely,
Whatsoever things are of good report;
think on these things.
—Philippians 4:8—

C. Read the groups of words below. Some of them are sentences. Some of them are phrases. Make the phrases into sentences by adding more words. On your paper write the sentences you make.

1. Peter was in prison.
2. An angel came to him.
3. opened the door.
4. The angel led Peter outside.
5. knocked on a door.
6. The people were praying.
7. They were glad to see Peter.
8. They thanked

D. Go back and check your work. Check for these things.

1. Is every sentence a complete thought?
2. Does every sentence begin with a capital letter?
3. Does every sentence end with the proper mark?

16. More About Answering Questions

An asking sentence is a **question**. We use words to build questions. Read this question. Count the words.

Who made the animals?

There are four words in this question. This is an easy question. We know the answer to this question.

God

We learned that we should use complete sentences to answer questions. The word **God** is not a sentence. Let us write a telling sentence to answer our question.

God made the animals.

This is a good answer. This sentence tells us who made the animals. Look at the words in the answer. Do you see the words that are also in the question? We used three words from the question to help write the answer.

Who **made the animals?**
God **made the animals.**

Read these questions and answers:

Who **obeyed God?**
Abraham **obeyed God.**
Who **was a shepherd?**
David **was a shepherd.**

Do you see which words are alike in each pair? Do you see which words are different?

> Remember: When we write answers, we use words from the question to help us. The words used in a question help us build our answers.

▷ For You to Do ▷

Copy each pair of sentences below. Choose a good word to answer each question. Use this word to complete the telling sentence. Then draw a circle around the words in the question that are used in the telling sentence. The first one is done for you.

1. Who made us?
   God made us.
2. Who loves us?
   — loves us.
3. Who walked on water?
   — walked on water.
4. Who prayed to God?
   — prayed to God.
5. What can fly?
   — can fly.
6. What ran away?
   — ran away.

17. Writing Our Answers

God wants us to learn to write. He wants us to learn to write good sentences. He wants us to learn to write good answers. We must practice writing good answers. Read this question.

Who built the ark?

This question asks who did something. What did somebody do?

built the ark

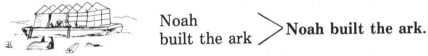

This is what somebody did. These words are in the question. Point to these words in the question. We will use these words to help build our answer.

Did you know **who** built the ark? We know that Noah did. We will use the word **Noah** to help build our answer. Let us put our words together.

Noah
built the ark > **Noah built the ark.**

Read the sentence above. Does the sentence answer the question? This is a good answer because it tells us who built the ark.

Read the sentences below.

Who made a golden calf?
Moses made a golden calf.
Aaron was the high priest.
Aaron made a golden calf.

Which answer is a good answer? The first answer is not true. Moses did not make a golden calf. The second sentence is true, but it does not answer the question. The third sentence is a good answer. It is a true answer. It tells us who made the golden calf.

> For You to Do >

Copy the questions below. Skip a line between each question. Underline the words in the question that you will use to help build your answer. Then write your answer in a complete sentence on the line under each question.

1. Who goes to school?
2. Who cooks supper?
3. Who plays with toys?

> More Practice and Review >

The sentences below are not complete. Use words or phrases to complete them. Write the complete sentences on your paper.

1. —— is ringing.   4. —— grew.
2. The people ——.   5. God ——.
3. —— is waiting.   6. The moon ——.

18. Changing Word Order

We can use the words in a question to help us write a good answer. We write the answer in a telling sentence. Read these sentences:

Who **followed Jesus?**
Andrew **followed Jesus.**

Which words in the question did we use when we wrote our answer? We wrote these words in the same order as in the question. We did not change where these words were in the sentence. Now read the sentences below.

Where **is Mother?**
Mother is at home.

Do you see the words from the question which we used in the answer? Are they in the same order? No, we had to change where these words were in the sentence. It would not be right to say: **At home is Mother.** This sentence would sound strange. The words would not be in correct order.

We must be careful to write our answers properly. We must write our words in correct order.

> The questions we ask,
> The answers we write:
> Let the words be in order,
> With all things done right.

> **For You to Do** >

Copy the questions and incomplete sentences below. In each question circle the words which will be used in the answer. Then choose a good word or phrase to complete each telling sentence. The first one is done for you.

1. Where ⟨is⟩ ⟨Jesus⟩?
   Jesus is *in heaven* .

2. Where are the birds?
   The birds are ——.

3. Where was the boat?
   The boat was ——.

4. What day is today?
   Today is ——.

> **More Practice and Review** >

From each set below copy the answer that is a good answer. Remember to use the rules you learned about the beginning and ending of a sentence.

1. Who praised God?
   Simeon
   Simeon praised God

2. Who sang songs?
   Paul was in prison
   Paul sang songs

3. What did Moses see?
   Moses saw a burning bush
   a burning bush Moses saw

19. Writing More Answers

We have rules to help us write good answers. Read these rules:

1. Read the question carefully.
2. Choose which words you will use to help write the answer.
3. Choose a good word or phrase which **tells** what the sentence **asks**.
4. Write the answer clearly in a complete telling sentence.
5. Check to see if the words are in correct order.
6. Read the question and answer together. Be certain that the answer is a good answer for the question asked.

Rules 5 and 6 are very important. We must always check our work. We must be certain that we did not make any mistakes.

Only God is perfect. Only God never makes any mistakes. When God made everything, He saw that it was good. He did not need to check His work.

We must check our own work. We must look for mistakes. At home, our parents check our work. They tell us if we did not do something well. We listen to what they tell us. Then we correct what we did wrong.

In school, the teacher checks our work also. She helps us find any mistakes we did not see. We should listen carefully and then correct the mistakes she shows us.

➤ For You to Do ➤

Copy each question below. Underline the words you will use to help write your answer. Then write your answer in a complete sentence.

1. Where is the baby?
2. Whose cows are those?
3. Where was Joseph?
4. Where are we?
5. When will we sing?

➤ More Practice and Review ➤

Follow the rules to help answer the questions below. Use your lesson to help find the answers.

1. Who is perfect?
2. Who did not check His work?
3. Who can make mistakes?
4. What must we look for?
5. Who helps us check our work?

20. Reviewing What We Have Learned

A. Copy each question and incomplete sentence below. Circle the words in the question which are used to help build the answer. Be ready to say whether these words had to change order. Use the words at the right to complete each telling sentence correctly.

1. Who was Moses' sister?   **in a basket**
   —— was Moses' sister.

2. Where was Baby Moses?   **The princess**
   Baby Moses was ——.

3. Who found Baby Moses?   **Moses' brother**
   —— found Baby Moses.

4. Whose brother was Aaron?   **Miriam**
   Aaron was ——.

B. Write a good answer for each question below. Follow the rules given in lesson 19.

1. Who teaches school?
2. Where is Jesus?
3. What is your name?
4. What has feathers?
5. Who made the trees?

C. Below are four questions. Under each question are two answers. On your paper write **a** or **b** to tell which answer is a good answer and is written correctly.

1. Who answered the door?
   a. Rhoda did.
   b. Rhoda answered the door.
2. Who was knocking?
   a. Peter
   b. Peter was knocking.
3. Where had he been?
   a. He had been in prison.
   b. In prison had he been.
4. Whose house was it?
   a. it was Mary's house
   b. It was Mark's mother's house.

D. Be ready to say what was wrong with the answers above which you did not choose. Use this checklist to help you.

1. Sentence must be complete.
2. Sentence must begin and end correctly.
3. Sentence must tell what happened.
4. Words must be in correct order.

21. A Proper Order

God is a God of **order**. He has made a right way for everything to be done. He has made everything happen in its right way.

God wants us to do things in proper **order** also. He wants us to do everything at the right time and in the right way. God wants our sentences to be in order. He wants us to write sentences that show good word order.

Read these sentences:

Prayed to God Jacob. Down lay he.

Can you understand these sentences? No, the words are not in good order. They are confusing. When we write sentences, we must put our words in good order. Now read these sentences:

Jacob prayed to God. He lay down.

We can understand these sentences. The words are in good order. They are not confusing.

Read the Bible verse at the bottom of this page. This verse tells us that we must do everything in the right way. We must do everything in a way that pleases God. This is a good Bible verse to learn. Memorize this verse.

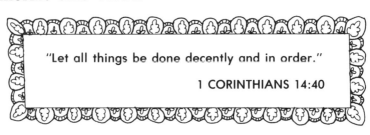

"Let all things be done decently and in order."

1 CORINTHIANS 14:40

> **For You to Do** >

Next to each number below are two groups of words. One of the groups of words is not in proper order. Copy the group of words that is in proper order. Use capital letters and proper end marks.

1. loves me God
   God loves me

2. is Jesus where now
   where is Jesus now

3. God's Word is true
   true God's Word is

4. she home came
   she came home

5. who ate manna
   manna ate who

6. songs we sing
   we sing songs

> **More Practice and Review** >

A. How should everything be done?

B. Choose a good word to complete these sentences.

1. — is cold.
2. I saw —.
3. We ate —.
4. The dog —.
5. — ran home.

C. Check your work. Did you use a complete sentence to answer the question in part A?

22. Putting Words in Order

Sometimes words are not in good order. Sometimes we must put words in good order. Look at these words:

games James played.

These words are confusing. They do not form a good sentence. We must put these words in good order. Whom do you think the sentence is about?

James

This is the first word in our sentence. Which word tells us what James did?

played

Now we can say: James played. There is still one word left. This word tells us what James played.

James played games.

Now our words are in good order. Now they form a good sentence.

To put words in order, decide which word tells whom or what the sentence is about. Then find the word which tells what the first word did or is doing. Put any other words where they make the best sense in the sentence.

> For You to Do >

Put these words in order to form good sentences. Write the sentences on your paper.

1. prayed Jacob
2. sang birds
3. sings who
4. read we the Bible
5. songs I sing

6. to church go we
7. are the books where
8. is bright the sun
9. sweet honey is
10. was green the grass

> More Practice and Review >

A. Copy the groups of words which are sentences. Begin and end them properly.

1. farmer plowing
2. the girl is reading
3. the wind is blowing
4. flowers tall
5. the trees have fruit

B. Match the words and phrases from each column to form a sentence. Write each sentence on your paper.

A	B
the boat	helped sing
the children	check our work
where	is kind
God	was old
we	is Father

23. Making Sentences

God made us in a wonderful way. Our eyes can see. Our minds help us know what our eyes see. We use our tongues to say what we see. We can use our hands to write what we see. We make many sentences about the things we see.

Look at this picture.
What do you see?
We see a **boy.**

We will write a sentence about this boy. **Boy** will be one word in our sentence.

Look at the picture again. What is the boy doing?
fishing

Now we have two words for our sentence.

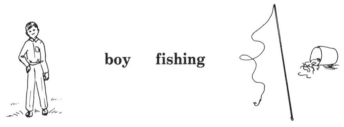

boy   fishing

Is "Boy fishing" a sentence? No, we need to use more words. How would we say this?

The boy is fishing.

We added two little words. Point to the words we added. We needed to use these words to help build a good sentence. These words help us say and write what our eyes see. These words help us write a complete thought.

For You to Do

Write a sentence about each picture below. Use these steps to help you:

1. Decide what or whom the picture is about.
2. Decide what is happening.
3. Use these two words or phrases as the sentence base.
4. Add any other words needed to help make a complete thought.
5. Check your work.

1.

2.

3.

4.

5.

6.

7.

8.

24. Writing More Sentences

God gave us wonderful eyes. Our eyes can see many things. We see many things at one time. Right now your eyes are seeing this page. But they do not just see a piece of paper. Your eyes see words. They see many words. They see periods and capital letters. Together these things make one picture.

Look at this picture: Many things are happening in this picture. What do you see happening?

Two kittens are playing.
One kitten is sleeping.
A mother cat is watching.

Can you see anything else happening in the picture? Can you find the sentences below in the picture?

A girl is swinging.
Flowers are blooming.

God wants us to use the gifts He gave us. He wants us to use our eyes in a good way. He wants us to use our eyes to see the many things He has made.

"Come and see the works of God"
Psalm 66:5

> For You to Do >

Study the big picture in the center of this page. What do you see? Write five sentences about what you see.

> More Practice and Review >

A. Below are five groups of words. Use the words in each group to form a good sentence.

1. Paul
   in
   God
   trusted

2. obeyed
   he
   God

3. went
   Rome
   to
   he

4. by
   boat
   he
   travelled

5. storm
   big
   was
   a
   there

B. Check all your work. Are all the words in proper order? Does every sentence make sense? Does every sentence begin and end properly?

25. Reviewing What We Have Learned

A. Write from memory the Bible verse which tells how all things should be done.

B. Below are five groups of words. They are not sentences. Add words to each group to make a sentence. Write the five sentences on your paper.

1. men praying
2. people listening
3. child throwing ball
4. what very tall
5. small flower yellow

C. Write a good word to complete each sentence below.

1. A —— is a complete thought.
2. We use our —— to see.
3. We use our —— to write what we see.
4. We use —— and —— to build sentences.
5. Our words must be in proper ——.

D. Look at the pictures below. Write a good sentence to go with each picture.

1.   5.

2.   6.

3.   7.

4.   8.

E. Look around your classroom. Write five sentences about what you see.

F. Check all your work. Check for these things:

  1. Is every sentence a complete thought?
  2. Does every sentence begin and end properly?
  3. Are the words in proper order?
  4. Are the words kind and true?
  5. Are the words spelled correctly?
  6. Is your work done neatly?

Review One

A. Answer these questions.

1. What is a sentence?
2. How should we begin every sentence?
3. What are two marks that we use at the end of sentences?

B. Read the groups of words below. Tell whether each group is a **sentence** or a **phrase**.

1. David was a shepherd
2. One day Samuel
3. Whose son was he
4. Jesse his father
5. Who was the king
6. Saul was the king
7. Jonathan was Saul's son
8. Were friends
9. David and Jonathan
10. Where did Saul live

C. Tell whether each sentence in part B **tells** or **asks**. Then tell what mark you would put at the end of each sentence.

D. Add words to the phrases in part B to make complete sentences.

> **Written Practice** >

A. On your paper write the word which would best complete each sentence below.

| kind | capital | words | telling |
| phrase | please | sentence | asking |

1. A —— is a complete thought.
2. A —— is not a complete thought.
3. A —— sentence ends with a period.
4. An —— sentence ends with a question mark.
5. Every sentence begins with a —— letter.
6. We use —— and phrases to build sentences.
7. Our words should be —— and true.
8. Our sentences should —— God.

B. Write from memory 1 Corinthians 14:40. This verse tells how all things should be done.

C. Some of the groups of words below are phrases, and some of them are sentences. Find the sentences and write them correctly.

1. who goes to school
2. Mary and I
3. we study our lessons
4. Sister Anna teaches us
5. brought our lunch
6. what do you read

Review Two

Oral Drill

A. Use a word which tells **who** or **what** to complete each sentence below.

1. —— roared.
2. —— swim.
3. —— rang.
4. —— played.
5. —— smiled.
6. —— saw Lois.
7. —— helped us.
8. —— ran fast.
9. —— are soft.
10. —— tastes sweet.

B. Use a word which tells what someone or something **does** or **did** to complete each sentence below.

1. The boys ——.
2. John and Lee ——.
3. Anne and Joy ——.
4. Little kittens ——.
5. Some birds ——.
6. We ——.
7. They ——.
8. Balls ——.
9. Wind ——.
10. Stars ——.

C. Put the words in each group below in correct order to make a sentence.

1. the   lawn   James   mowed
2. is   where   the   sun
3. barked   brown   dogs   the
4. made   us   who

⊳ Written Practice ⊳

A. Write a complete sentence to answer each question below.

1. What is your name?
2. Who is your teacher?
3. Where are the birds?
4. What did you see?

B. Add words to each group below to make a complete sentence. Write each sentence correctly.

1. baby playing
2. large horse black
3. where Mother

C. Change the order of the words in each group below to make a sentence. Write each sentence correctly.

1. Father   the   boys   did   find
2. the   dog   black   large   is

D. By changing the word order, the words in part C can be used to make several different sentences. How many sentences can you make from each group of words?

Extra Activity

Making a Booklet

Cut a piece of heavy paper into six equal pieces. Staple the six pieces together to form a booklet.

Number the pages 1-12.

On page one, write "What I Do in School."

On the odd number pages (3, 5, 7, 9, and 11), write sentences which tell what you do in school.

On the even number pages (2, 4, 6, 8, and 10), paste or draw pictures to go with your sentences.

Leave page 12 blank.

Take your booklet home to your parents.

A Poem to Enjoy

The Little Things

Little drops of water,
  Little grains of sand,
Make the mighty ocean
  And the pleasant land.

Little deeds of kindness,
  Little words of love,
Make our earth an Eden
Like the heaven above.

—Julia Fletcher Carney

Discussing the poem:

1. Could one drop of water make an ocean?
2. Could one grain of sand make the land?
3. When we say that a place is like Eden, we mean that it is a pleasant place. What makes the earth a pleasant place?
4. Do our deeds and words have to be big?
5. How many of them do you think there should be?

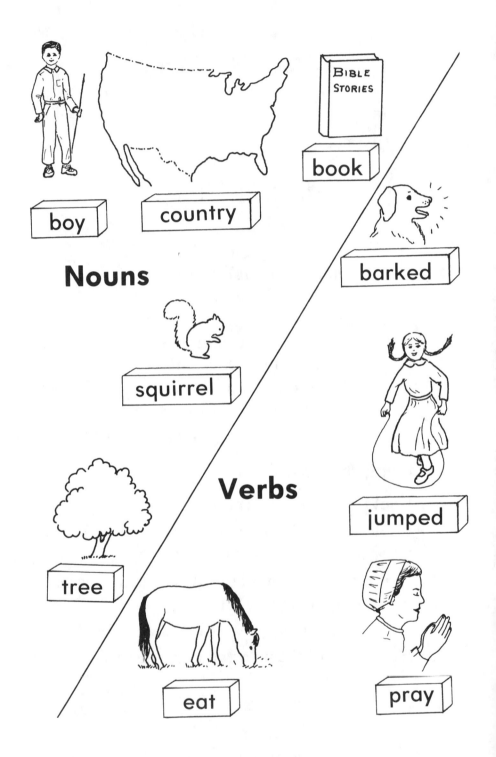

Nouns

boy

country

book

squirrel

tree

Verbs

barked

jumped

eat

pray

Unit II

Basic Building Blocks
of Our Language

"A word spoken in due season,
how good is it!"

Proverbs 15:23

1. Naming Words

God gave every person or thing something to do. He gave each thing a special kind of work. Even words have work to do. God made many kinds of words. Each kind of word has a different work.

Look at these words:

mother   town   camel   table

These words all have the same kind of work. Their work is to **name**. They name **people**, **places**, and **things**. We can call these words **naming words**.

Look at the pictures below. Read the word under each picture. Each word names what you see in the picture. Each of these words is a **naming word**.

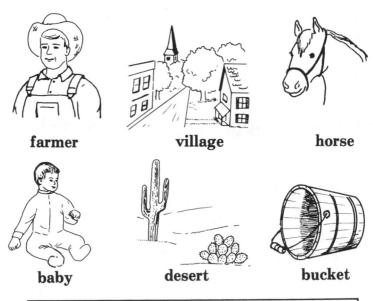

farmer   **village**   **horse**

baby   **desert**   **bucket**

Remember: Naming words name people, places, and things.

> For You to Do >

A. On your paper write a naming word to name what you see in each picture below.

1.

4.

7.

2.

5.

8.

3.

6.

9.

B. The sentences below are not complete. Use a naming word to complete each sentence. Write the complete sentences on your paper.

1. The —— broke.
2. An —— is red.
3. Many —— sang.
4. —— made us.
5. We went to ——.
6. The —— cried.
7. This is a ——.
8. He threw a ——.
9. Jesus is in ——.
10. —— came home.

2. Nouns

God made many things. Everything God made has a name. Every person and place God made has a name. We use naming words to name all the things God has made.

Naming words have a name, too. We call naming words **nouns**. We use nouns to help build sentences.

Look at these sentences:

Frogs croaked.
Bees buzzed.

Can you find the nouns in these sentences? **Frogs** and **bees** are both nouns. These words name things we can see and touch.

Some nouns name things we cannot see. Read the words below.

peace   joy   faith

These words are nouns. They name things we cannot see or touch. God has made many things we cannot see. We use nouns to name the things we can see and the things we cannot see.

God used many nouns in the Bible. Some of the nouns God used name things we can see. Some of the nouns God used name things we cannot see. God used all the nouns to help build sentences.

Remember: Words that name are called **nouns**.

For You to Do

Read the words below. All of these words are nouns. We can find these nouns in the Bible. Some of them name things we can see. Some of them name things we cannot see. Make two columns on your paper. Label one column **Things We Can See.** Label the other column **Things We Cannot See.** Write each noun in the proper column.

tree	children	earth	meekness
fish	shepherd	eyes	fruit
boat	mercy	grace	goodness
faith	wings	crown	mountain
city	fathers	peace	charity

More Practice and Review

Copy each sentence. Circle the noun in each.

1. Horses trot.
2. Children play.
3. Mother smiled.
4. The grass is tall.
5. A dish is broken.
6. This town is small.
7. Please sweep the floor.
8. Check your work.
9. Peace be with you.
10. Speak the truth.

3. Nouns That Tell *Who*

Nouns name people, places, and things. We use nouns to build sentences. We use nouns to answer questions. Read these questions and answers:

Who prayed?   **Peter** prayed.
Who spoke?   The **minister** spoke.
Who sang?   The **children** sang.

These questions all ask **who** did something. Each answer tells who did it. Point to the word in each answer which names who did something. Each of these words is a noun. Each of these nouns names a person.

> **Nouns that name people answer the question who.**

Read the nouns below. These nouns name people.

farmer	father	James	Sarah	children
baker	mother	John	Martha	men
pilot	sister	Mark	Lois	brethren
teacher	baby	Luke	Ruth	women

> **For You to Do** >

Using the list from the previous page, find a noun which tells:

1. who raises corn
2. who sleeps in a crib
3. who is a boy
4. who is a girl
5. who would be more than one person

> **More Practice and Review** >

A. On your paper write the noun which tells **who** in each sentence below.

1. Joann smiled.
2. Boys colored.
3. Mother sewed.
4. The girl made dinner.
5. Jesse played.
6. Children helped.
7. The minister spoke.
8. Paul came home.
9. Jesus wept.
10. Brother John sang.

B. Use a noun that tells **who** to answer the questions below. Write your answers in complete sentences.

1. Who taught school?
2. Who went to Sunday school?
3. Who plays with the ball?
4. Who made the world?

4. Nouns That Tell *What*

We learned that nouns that tell who name people. Now we will learn about the nouns that tell **what**. Read these questions and answers:

What roared?   A **lion** roared.
What fell?   **Leaves** fell.

These questions ask **what** did something. Each answer tells what did it. Point to the word in each answer which names what did something. Each of these words is a noun. Each of these nouns names a **thing**.

Nouns that name things answer the question what.

God has created many things. He created them out of nothing. God gave man the wisdom to know how to make things. When man makes something, he must use things that God created. Look at the pictures below. Some of the things were created by God. Some of the things were made by man.

≥ For You to Do ≥

Make two columns on your paper. Label the first one **What God Created**. Label the second one **What Man Made**. Using the pictures at the bottom of the previous page, list five things God created. Then list five things man made.

≥ More Practice and Review ≥

A. Find the nouns that tell **what** in the sentences and phrases below. Write these nouns on your paper.

1. in the box
2. Geese honked.
3. under the bed
4. Pigeons flew.
5. on the table

6. The flowers are red.
7. Do you want an orange?
8. Open the door.
9. Where is the book?
10. The bird pecked John.

B. Use nouns that name things to answer the questions below. Write your answers in complete sentences.

1. What swims?
2. What flies?
3. What do we sit on?
4. What do we eat?

5. Reviewing What We Have Learned

A. In a complete sentence tell what nouns do.

B. Look at the picture below. On your paper write ten nouns that you can see in the picture.

C. Make two columns on your paper. Label one column **Who**. Label the other column **What**. Put each noun below in the proper column.

mother	house	grandfather
beans	dress	dictionary
grass	uncle	giraffe
Jacob	paper	Solomon
stove	Adam	minister

D. The sentences below are written in the Bible. Find the noun in each sentence. Write the noun on your paper.

1. Obey your parents.
2. He restoreth my soul.
3. The ungodly are not so.
4. I will lift up mine eyes.
5. Blessed are the meek.
6. My cup runneth over.
7. My peace I leave with you.
8. His mercy endureth for ever.
9. His leaf also shall not wither.
10. Where is the lamb?

E. Use complete sentences to answer these questions. Underline the noun in each answer.

1. Who sang?
2. What sings?
3. Who ran?
4. What runs?
5. Who laughed?

6. Telling *Who* and *What*

Read these questions and answers:

> **Who** threw a ball?   **John** threw a ball.
> **What** did John throw?   John threw a **ball**.

The first question asks **who**. The second question asks **what**. The answer is the same telling sentence for both questions. This telling sentence tells **who** and **what**.

Many sentences tell who and what. A sentence which tells who and what has two nouns. One noun names a person. One noun names a thing.

Look at the two nouns in each of these sentences. Which noun names a person? Which noun names a thing?

> **Father** milks the **cows**.
> The **boys** found a **turtle**.
> A **wasp** stung **Lois**.

When you read a sentence, ask yourself which word tells who. Then ask yourself which word tells what. This will help you find the nouns in a sentence.

Remember: If nouns name people they tell who. If nouns name things they tell what.

> For You to Do >

Each sentence below has two nouns. Write the nouns on your paper. After each noun write **who** if it answers the question **who**. Write **what** if the noun tells **what**.

1. Sarah cooked supper.
2. The men ate the food.
3. Mary rode on a donkey.
4. The donkey carried Mary.
5. Zacchaeus climbed a tree.
6. The leaves did not hide Zacchaeus.
7. Jesus saw Zacchaeus.
8. Father mended the chair.
9. The fire burned the wood.
10. Ruth dried the dishes.

> More Practice and Review >

Use nouns to help answer these questions. Write your answers in complete sentences.

1. Who teaches school?
2. What bit Carl?
3. Who read the story?
4. What does a rabbit eat?
5. What swims in the sea?

7. Nouns That Tell *What Place*

God has made many people and things. We use nouns to name the many people and things God has made. God has made many places also. We can use nouns to name the many places God has made.

Read these questions and answers:

> **What place** did God promise to Abraham?
> God promised **Canaan** to Abraham.
> In **what place** was Moses born?
> Moses was born in **Egypt**.

These questions ask **what place**. The word in each answer which tells **what place** is a noun. Each of these nouns is a name of a place.

Here are some more nouns which name places:

Jerusalem	Babylon	city
Nazareth	Rome	country
Bethlehem	Judea	town

Nouns that name places answer the question what place.

> For You to Do >

Use a noun from the list to complete each sentence below. Write the complete sentences correctly.

1. An —— is a large body of water.
2. A small —— is on our farm.
3. —— is a country.
4. Many tall buildings are in the ——.
5. A —— is not as large as a city.
6. Did you ever visit the state of ——?

city   pond   Ohio   ocean   town   Mexico

> More Practice and Review >

Find the nouns in the sentences below. Write the nouns on your paper. After each noun write whether it tells **who** or **what**. Some sentences have two nouns.

1. The teacher watched.
2. The children played tag.
3. One girl fell.
4. Karen spoke gently.
5. Her words were gentle.
6. Jason tagged Paul.
7. Sister Ann rang the bell.
8. The boys and girls went inside.

8. *Who, What,* **and** *What Place*

How many nouns can one sentence have? Some sentences have only one noun. Some sentences have two nouns. Read the sentence below. It is a sentence from the Bible.

> "And God remembered Noah, and every living thing, and all the cattle that was with him in the ark: and God made a wind to pass over the earth, and the waters asswaged."
>
> (Genesis 8:1)

There are nine nouns in the above sentence. Can you find all of them?

It is wonderful how God has made our language. We can write a sentence which tells one or two things, or we can write a sentence which tells many things.

Read these sentences:

> Moses carried his **rod** to **Egypt**.
> **Paul** wrote a **letter** to **Rome**.
> **John** ate **locusts** in the **wilderness**.

Each of these sentences tells three things: who, what, and what place. Each sentence has three nouns.

Who	What	What Place
Moses	rod	Egypt
Paul	letter	Rome
John	locusts	wilderness

> For You to Do >

Make three columns on your paper as shown below. Then write the nouns for each sentence in the proper column. The first one is done for you.

Example: <u>Who</u>   <u>What</u>   <u>What Place</u>
          Abraham   flocks   Canaan

1. Abraham took his flocks to Canaan.
2. Lot pitched his tent toward Sodom.
3. God rained fire upon the plain.
4. The Hebrews made bricks in Goshen.
5. The women sang a song in the wilderness.
6. A prophet took a ship to Tarshish.
7. Ruth gathered grain near Bethlehem.
8. Solomon built a temple in Jerusalem.
9. His wives worshiped idols in the city.
10. Jesus broke bread by the seaside.

> More Practice and Review >

Copy the sentences below correctly. Underline any nouns. Be ready to tell what question each noun answers.

1. joseph found his brothers in Dothan
2. merchants bought the boy
3. the camels were bearing spices to Egypt
4. joseph had a coat
5. his brothers took the coat home

9. Finding Nouns as We Read

How good a spoonful of honey is! How pleasant the sticky sweetness tastes in our mouth as we carefully lick every drop from the spoon! We always eat it slowly enough that we can taste every bit of the good sweetness. But we try not to eat it so slowly that some of the honey drips away.

God gave us honey. God is glad that we enjoy its sweetness. Did you know that God also gave us something that is even sweeter than honey?

"How sweet are thy words unto my taste!
Yea, sweeter than honey to my mouth!"
(Psalm 119:103)

Yes, God's Word is even sweeter than honey. When we read His Word we should be careful to get all the good sweetness we can. We must not read so quickly that we miss the important truths God wants to teach us. Nor should we read so slowly that our minds wander and bits of truth slip away.

We should learn to ask ourselves questions while we read. Then we can tell others what we have read. Then we can answer their questions.

Three questions we can ask ourselves are **who, what,** and **where.** As we ask **who** we will remember the people in the story. As we ask **what** we will remember the things in the story. As we ask **where,** we will remember the places in the story. Learn to ask yourself these questions while you read.

For You to Do

Read Acts 10:1-8. Ask yourself **who, what,** and **where** as you read. Then shut your Bible and answer the questions below.

1. Whom is the story about?
2. Whom did the man fear?
3. What did the man give to the people?
4. Who came to the man in a vision?
5. Where did the man send his servants?

More Practice and Review

A. Copy the Bible verse from your lesson. Memorize this verse.

B. Make three columns on your paper:

Who   What   Where

Find the nouns in the sentences below and write each noun in the correct column.

1. Peter was in the city.
2. The disciple saw a great sheet.
3. The cloth held many animals.
4. Peter left Joppa and went to Caesarea.
5. Cornelius believed God.

10. Reviewing What We Have Learned

A. Write from memory Psalm 119:103.

B. Make three columns on your paper:

Who   What   Where

Find the nouns in the sentences below and write each noun in the proper column.

1. God spoke to Jonah.
2. The prophet did not obey the command.
3. The man took a ship to Tarshish.
4. There was a storm at sea.
5. The waves frightened the sailors.
6. The men drew lots.
7. Jonah was cast into the sea.
8. God sent a fish to swallow Jonah.
9. The whale spewed Jonah out onto dry ground.
10. Then Jonah went to Nineveh.
11. The people in this city listened.
12. Jonah made a booth.
13. God caused a gourd to grow.
14. A worm ate the gourd.
15. God taught Jonah a lesson.

C. Study the picture on this page. Use nouns you see in the picture to help you answer the questions below. Write your answers in complete sentences. Then underline all the nouns in your sentences.

1. Who is walking on the grass?
2. Where are they going?
3. Who is carrying the lunch pail?
4. What is the girl picking?
5. Who is petting the dog?
6. Who is standing at the door?
7. What is she ringing?
8. Who must hurry?

Read your sentences. Do they make a story?

11. Writing Names of *People*

God named the first man Adam. Then God told Adam to name the woman and all the animals. Adam named his wife Eve. When Adam wanted to talk to his wife, he did not say, "woman." He said, "Eve." Eve did not call her husband, "man." She called him, "Adam."

When God gave Adam and Eve two sons, they named them also. They named one Cain and one Abel. If they wanted to call both of their sons, they could say, "boys." But if they wanted to call only one son, they could not just say, "boy." They had to say "Cain" or "Abel." They had to say the name of the specific boy they wanted.

What does your teacher call you? Does she say "boy"? or "girl"? No, there are many boys and girls. Your teacher says your name. Then everybody knows which specific boy or girl she wants.

When we write the name of a specific person, we must follow a special rule. We must begin the name with a capital letter. Look at the names below. Each of them begins with a capital letter. Each of them names a specific person.

Jacob   Hannah   Timothy   Karen   William

Remember: Names of specific people begin with a capital letter.

> For You to Do >

A. Write the specific name for:

1. each of the boys in your class
2. each of the girls in your class
3. your teacher
4. the children in your family

B. Use a name from the list below to name the specific person suggested by each definition. Begin each name with a capital letter.

1. a man who walked with God   (Genesis 5:22)
2. a man who was very tall   (1 Samuel 17:4)
3. a woman who helped others   (Acts 9:36)
4. the mother of Timothy   (2 Timothy 1:5)
5. a daughter of Saul   (1 Samuel 18:20)

   goliath   michal   dorcas   enoch   eunice

12. Writing Names of *Places*

Where did God tell Joseph to take Mary and Baby Jesus? Did He just tell him to go to another country? No, God wanted Joseph to go to a specific country. He told Joseph to take the mother and child to Egypt.

What did the angel tell Cornelius? Did the angel tell Cornelius to send his servants to just any town to find Peter? No, the angel named a specific town. He named the town of Joppa.

Egypt is the name of a specific country. Joppa is the name of a specific town. There are many places in the world, and each place has its own special name. We use these names to say which specific place we mean.

Read the names of the specific places listed below. Each name begins with a capital letter.

country	state	city	river
Mexico	Iowa	Lancaster	Jordan
India	Kansas	Ottawa	Nile
Canada	Ohio	Chicago	Hudson

> Remember: Names of specific places begin with a capital letter.

> For You to Do >

A. Write correctly the name for the specific:

1. town or city you live near
2. state or province in which you live
3. country in which you live

B. Write correctly the name of a specific:

1. river
2. country where you do not live
3. town in your state or province
4. state or province where you do not live

(Use a map if you need help).

> More Practice and Review >

Find the two nouns in each sentence below. Write them correctly on your paper. After each noun write whether it names a specific **person** or a specific **place**.

1. moses went to midian.
2. joshua crossed the jordan.
3. paul went to rome.
4. david lived at ziklag.
5. bethany was the home of lazarus.

13. Writing Proper Nouns

The name of a specific person or place is called a **proper noun**. Whenever we say **Sarah, Paul,** or **Timothy** we are using a **proper noun**. Whenever we say **New York, Manitoba,** or **China** we are using a **proper noun**.

Many nouns are not proper nouns. The word **town** is a noun, but it does not name a specific place. The word **town** is not a proper noun. Nouns that are not proper nouns are called **common nouns**.

Common nouns and **proper** nouns are the two main groups of nouns. Read the examples in each group below.

Common	Proper
town	Carlton
school	Hope Christian Day School
church	Clover Mennonite Church
country	India
boy	Thomas
woman	Mrs. Mary Hoover

Look at the common nouns. They do not begin with a capital letter. Now look at the proper nouns. Every proper noun begins with a capital letter.

Some of the proper nouns have more than one word. Look at each word in the name. Each word in the proper noun begins with a capital letter.

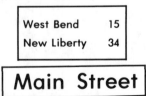

Joywood Mennonite Church

| West Bend | 15 |
| New Liberty | 34 |

Main Street

> **For You to Do**

Write these proper nouns correctly:

1. guatemala
2. mexico city
3. quebec
4. north dakota
5. mount sinai
6. brother jacob horst
7. mississippi river
8. blue ridge mountains
9. valley mennonite church
10. joy christian day school

> **More Practice and Review**

Write correctly:

1. your full name
2. your teacher's name
3. the name of your school
4. the name of your church
5. the names of the people in your family

Sandra King
Menno Baker
Joyce Brown
Becky Smith

14. Recognizing Proper Nouns

God wants us to do our work well. We must take time to do our work well. We must not hurry with our work and do it in a way that is careless and displeasing to God. Nor should we do our work too slowly. If we work too slowly, our minds will wander, and we will forget the work we are supposed to be doing. When we work we must think about what we are doing. We must think about doing our work in a way that will please God.

Writing is one kind of work which God has given us to do. When we write, we must think about the words we write. We must also remember the rules which we should follow.

Here are some rules to follow when we write:

1. Write each letter of each word neatly.
2. Spell each word correctly.
3. Write sentences that are true and kind.
4. Write answers in complete sentences.
5. Begin and end sentences correctly.
6. Begin every proper noun with a capital letter.
7. Check your work.

We must remember to watch for proper nouns when we are writing. We must remember that every noun which names a specific person or place is a proper noun. Every proper noun must begin with a capital letter.

> For You to Do >

Find the ten **proper** nouns in the list below. Write them correctly on your paper.

james	book	garden	israel
city	ohio	basket	river
lois	town	moses	montana
home	child	nevada	post office
john	ottawa	friend	north dakota

> More Practice and Review >

Answer these questions correctly, using what you have learned about writing good sentences.

1. Who is a girl in your class?
2. What is the name of your school?
3. Who is your minister?
4. What town do you live near?

15. Reviewing What We Have Learned

A. On your paper write the words which you would use to correctly complete the sentences below.

1. A —— names a person, place, or thing.
2. Nouns that name —— tell who.
3. Nouns that name —— tell what.
4. Nouns that name —— tell where.
5. The two main groups of nouns are —— and ——.
6. A —— noun does not name a specific person, place, or thing.
7. Every —— noun must begin with a capital letter.

B. Make three columns on your paper:

Who   What   Where

Find the nouns in the sentences below and write each noun in the correct column.

1. John carried the package to town.
2. A girl took her lunch to school.
3. The teacher read a story.
4. The children sang songs.
5. The class took a trip to the city.

C. Find ten proper nouns below. Write them correctly.

peace	north bend	table
susan	goodness	rome
vermont	menno simons	faith
geese	hudson bay	store
church	mr. smith	rivers
block	kindness	atlanta
joanna	sister martha	joy

D. Five of the nouns above name things we cannot see. Write these nouns on your paper.

E. Rewrite each sentence below leaving out the words in bold print type. Use a proper noun to take the place of the words you left out. The first one is done for you.

1. She went to **the city**.
   She went to **Trenton**.

2. **A boy** came home.

3. **The minister** spoke.

4. Carl went to **another country**.

5. **The teacher** teaches at **the school**.

16. *Doing* Words

God has made many kinds of words. Each kind of word has a special work to do. Some words, called nouns, name people, places, and things. Another kind of word is a **doing** word.

Read these two sentences:

Dogs bark.
A child helped.

Use a word from each sentence to answer these questions:

What do dogs **do?**
What did a child **do?**

Bark and **helped** are the **doing** words in the two sentences above. They tell what someone or something **does** or **did**.

A **doing** word tells what someone or something does or did.

Look at the pictures below. Read the sentence under each picture. Point to the word in each sentence which tells what someone or something is doing. This word is a **doing** word.

A horse runs.

Mary sews.

Remember: A doing word tells what someone or something does or did.

> **For You to Do** >

A. Choose a **doing** word from the list to complete each sentence by telling what each thing does. Write the complete sentences on your paper.

squawk   falls   blows   croak   swim
shine   bloom   sting   melts   roll

1. Fish ——.
2. Chickens ——.
3. Wind ——.
4. Balls ——.
5. Stars ——.

6. Rain ——.
7. Bees ——.
8. Frogs ——.
9. Flowers ——.
10. Ice ——.

B. In each sentence above, the **doing** word comes at the end of the sentence. When we give a command, we often put the **doing** word at the beginning of the sentence. On your paper write the **doing** word which is found in each command below.

1. Wash the dishes.
2. Open the door.
3. Study your lessons.
4. Walk quietly.

5. Sweep the floor.
6. Obey your parents.
7. Work carefully.
8. Speak kindly.

17. *Verbs*

Naming words are called nouns. Doing words have a special name also. We call doing words **verbs**. Every sentence needs to have a **verb**.

Read the groups of words below.

Sarah a book.
James the ball.

These groups of words are not sentences. They have no word to tell what somebody did or is doing. There is no **verb**.

What do you think Sarah might be doing? What do you think James is doing?

Sarah **reads** a book.
James **catches** the ball.

Now we know that Sarah is reading. We know that James is catching the ball. **Reads** and **catches** are good verbs to complete our sentences.

Sarah a book makes us think that Sarah might be reading. **James the ball** makes us think that James might be catching. Yet we would not know for certain.

Sarah **writes** a book.
James **throws** the ball.

Writes and **throws** are also two good verbs to complete the sentences. These words tell us something else that Sarah and James are doing.

When we write sentences we must use verbs. We must use verbs which tell exactly what someone or something does or did.

Remember: Doing words are called verbs.
Every sentence needs a verb.

> For You to Do >

Write each sentence two ways. Choose verbs from the list to help you complete each sentence.

knits   drove   gnawed   wears   eats
bakes   buried   entered   fixed   built

1. John —— the car.
2. Mother —— the cookies.
3. The dog —— a bone.
4. Noah —— the ark.
5. Grandmother —— a sweater.

> More Practice and Review >

Find the verb in each sentence below. Write the verbs on your paper.

1. Jesus healed.
2. The church prayed.
3. Zacchaeus climbed.
4. Peter spoke.
5. Praise God.
6. Who reads?
7. Many work.
8. Trust the Lord.

18. Finding Verbs

When we want to find a noun, we look for a word that names a person, place, or thing. When we want to find a verb, we look for a word that tells what someone does or did. We look for a word which shows **action.**

Look at the pictures below. Read the word underneath each picture. This word tells what **action** is taking place. Each of these words can be used as a verb.

write   jump   walk

pray   smile   sing

Many words can be used as verbs. To find a verb in a sentence ask: Which word tells what someone or something does or did? Which word shows action?

> For You to Do >

Find the verb in each sentence below. Write the verbs on your paper.

1. Joseph went to Bethlehem.
2. The donkey brayed.
3. An angel appeared to the shepherds.
4. The men listened.
5. A star shone in the sky.

> More Practice and Review >

A. Copy correctly the groups of words below which are complete sentences. Underline the verb in each.

1. samuel lay down
2. eli slept
3. the boy a fire
4. the boy heard a voice
5. he ran to Eli
6. susan the dishes
7. who spoke to Samuel
8. God talked to him
9. Jesus the children
10. Samuel listened

Do the sentences you wrote make a story?

B. Choose a good verb to complete the groups of words above which are not sentences. Write your complete sentences correctly.

19. Using Verbs

God made verbs. We use verbs to build sentences. We should be careful to build good sentences.

For our sentences to be good sentences, they must be accurate. Our sentences must tell exactly what happened. We use verbs to tell exactly what happened.

If you were playing a game of tag, and a person touched you, which one of these sentences would you say?

You **missed** me.
You **tagged** me.

The first sentence is not true because the verb does not tell what happened. The verb in the second sentence is accurate. It tells exactly what happened. This is the sentence you would say.

We should never say anything that is unkind or untrue. To speak the truth we must choose our words carefully. We must choose verbs which tell exactly what happened.

> For You to Do

Use a word from the list to complete the second sentence in each pair below. Make the second sentence say what happened in the first one. Write the sentences you complete on your paper.

1. Mother talked in a hushed voice.
Mother ——.

2. The boy sat patiently until Father came.
The boy —— for Father.

3. Father asked God to help us.
Father —— for help.

4. Sarah made a picture of a tree.
Sarah —— a tree.

5. The boy spoke in too loud a tone.
The boy ——.

prayed   whispered   drew   shouted   waited

More Practice and Review

A. Copy the verbs from the story below.

Jesus saw the fishermen. He called to them. They dropped their nets. Then they followed Jesus. Jesus made them fishers of men.

B. Write five sentences to tell five things you have done today. Underline the verb in each sentence.

20. Reviewing What We Have Learned

A. On your paper write the word or words which would correctly complete each sentence below.

1. —— made many kinds of words.
2. Naming words are called ——.
3. Doing words are called ——.
4. A doing word tells what someone or something —— or ——.

B. On your paper write the **doing** word which would best complete each sentence below. Use the Bible references to help you.

1. We should —— our parents.
2. We should —— without ceasing.
3. We should —— one another.
4. We should —— God for all things.
5. We should —— the truth in love.

Ephesians 6:1   1 Thessalonians 5:17

John 13:34   1 Thessalonians 5:18

Ephesians 4:15

> "Whether therefore ye eat, or drink, or whatsoever ye do, do all to the glory of God."
> 1 Corinthians 10:31

C. Find the verbs in the sentences below. Write the verbs on your paper.

1. The fruit ripened.
2. We picked the cherries.
3. Sarah pitted them.
4. Mother canned the fruit.
5. Who helped?
6. Martha and I washed the kettles.
7. Jacob carried the jars downstairs.
8. Sarah made three pies.
9. We each ate a piece.
10. In the evening, we rested.

D. Use a verb to complete each sentence. Write the complete sentences on your paper.

1. Children —— to school.
2. Jason —— the door.
3. Sister Anne ——.
4. We —— the Bible.
5. Who —— home?

21. Finding Nouns and Verbs

Did you ever go to a strange church? You saw many people sitting on the benches. Then one man stood up to preach. This man was the minister. You knew who he was by what he was doing. Another man taught Sunday school. You knew he was the teacher by what he was doing.

In a sentence, we can know whether a word is a noun or a verb by seeing what it does. Does the word name a person, place, or thing? Or does the word tell what somebody does or did?

Every sentence must have a verb. Most sentences have a noun, too. The noun tells whom or what the sentence is about.

Read the sentences below. Each one has a noun to tell whom or what the sentence is about. Point to the noun as you read each sentence.

Children sing.
Kittens play.

The first sentence is about **children**. **Children** is the noun in the first sentence. **Kittens** is a noun, too. The word **kittens** tells what the second sentence is about.

Is there a word in the first sentence which tells what children do? The verb **sing** tells what children do. In the second sentence, the verb **play** tells what kittens do.

> To know whether a word is a noun or a verb, we must know how it is being used in the sentence. If the word is naming a person, place, or thing, it is a noun. If the word is telling what somebody does or did, it is a verb.

⊳ For You to Do ⊳

A. Decide how the word in bold print is used in each sentence. Write **noun** or **verb** after each number on your paper.

1. Every Friday we **clean** the school.
2. Much **work** must be done.
3. We **help** the teacher.
4. The boys **empty** the wastebasket.
5. Some **girls** wipe the desks.
6. The **shelves** are dusted.
7. Who **sweeps** the floor?
8. Sometimes we **sing**.
9. Our **teacher** sings, too.
10. We all **work** cheerfully.

B. Copy these sentences. Circle the noun in each. Underline the verb.

1. The donkey balked.
2. A baby smiles.
3. The lion roars.
4. Check your work.
5. Open the door.
6. Sarah laughed.

22. Completing Sentences

Look at these two houses. They are not built correctly. They do not have all their parts. One house needs a door. The other one needs a roof.

When we build a sentence, we must be certain that it has everything it needs. Read the sentences below.

Prayed.
The three boys.

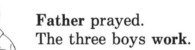

These sentences are not complete. They do not have everything they need. The first sentence does not have a noun to tell **who** prayed. The second sentence does not have a verb to tell us what the three boys **are doing.**

Father prayed.
The three boys **work.**

The noun **Father** makes the first sentence complete. The verb **work** completes the second sentence.

To complete a sentence, first find out what part is missing. Is there a noun to tell whom or what the sentence is about? Is there a verb to tell what happened? Choose a noun or verb which will make the sentence a complete thought.

► For You to Do ►

A. Read each sentence below. Decide whether the sentence needs a noun or a verb to make a complete thought. Choose a word from the correct list to supply the missing part. Write each sentence correctly.

1. Jesus ——.   **Nouns**
2. —— learn.   **children**
3. —— croak.   **thorns**
4. Bells ——.   **snow**
5. —— scratched.   **frogs**
6. Turkeys ——.   Verbs
7. Lightning ——.   **ring**
8. —— fell.   **flashed**
                      gobbled
                      wept

B. On your paper write how the word in bold print is used in each sentence. Write **noun** or **verb**.

1. **John** picked the corn.
2. Jacob and Martha **husked** it.
3. The **corn** tasted sweet.
4. The cows ate the **husks**.
5. Mother **froze** some corn.

23. Building Sentences

How does a carpenter build a house? Does he just take a pile of wood and hammer the pieces together quickly with some nails? No, the carpenter follows a plan. He works carefully and follows the plan which tells how the house should be built.

When we build a sentence, we must have a plan. We must decide what the sentence should say. We must choose our nouns and verbs carefully to build a good sentence which will say what we want. When we write the sentence, we must be careful to follow all the rules we have learned.

Susan wants to write a sentence. She wants to write a sentence about a small bird with a blue back and blue wings. She wants her sentence to say that this bird makes a pleasant musical sound.

Which of these nouns would Susan use to name her bird?

whale   cardinal   bluebird

Susan would choose the noun **bluebird** to tell what her sentence is about.

Now Susan must choose a verb to tell what the bluebird does.

squawks   pecks   sings

Sings is the verb which tells that the bluebird makes a musical sound.

The bluebird sings.

Susan followed the rules when she wrote her sentence. She used the little word **the** to help make the sentence complete. She put all the words in correct order. Susan started the sentence with a capital letter and ended it with a period. She wrote a good sentence.

> ⮞ **For You to Do** ⮞

A. Write ten sentences. Use a noun from the list to tell what the sentence is about. Use a verb from the list to tell what each thing does or did. Follow the rules to write good sentences.

Nouns		Verbs	
girls	eagles	trot	scurry
ponies	baby	soar	dripped
ball	glue	withered	work
star	rabbits	splashes	bounced
water	plants	stuck	twinkled

B. Write three sentences about what you see happening in your classroom. Circle the noun in each sentence. Underline the verb.

24. Looking at Sentences

Every sentence has two parts. The first part tells whom or what the sentence is about. The second part of the sentence always has a verb.

Jacob slept.

Jacob is a noun. It tells whom the sentence is about. **Slept** is a verb. It tells what Jacob did.

Some sentences tell about more than one person or thing.

<u>Adam</u> and <u>Eve</u> disobeyed.

This sentence tells about two people, **Adam** and **Eve**. These two nouns are both in the first part of the sentence.

Sometimes a sentence has more than one verb.

Daniel <u>fasted</u> and <u>prayed</u>.

Fasted and **prayed** are two verbs. They tell us that Daniel did two things. He **fasted**, and he **prayed**. **Fasted** and **prayed** are both in the second part of the sentence.

⊳ For You to Do ⊳

Some of the sentences below have only one noun or verb. Some of them have more than one noun or verb. Copy each sentence carefully. Draw a line between the nouns and verbs to show the two parts of the sentence. Then draw one line under each noun. Draw two lines under each verb. The first sentence is done for you.

1. <u>Boys</u> and <u>girls</u> | <u>work</u> and <u>play</u>.
2. Hannah prayed.
3. James and John fished.
4. Martha swept and dusted.
5. The dress tore.
6. Rain and sleet fell.
7. Ducks and swans swim and fly.
8. The glass slipped and broke.

⊳ More Practice and Review ⊳

A. Write two sentences using the noun **Mother** for the first part of each sentence. Use two different verbs to tell what **Mother** does. Draw a line between the two parts of each sentence.

B. Write two different sentences using the verb **fly**. Use different nouns to tell what things **fly**. Draw a line between the two parts of each sentence.

25. Reviewing What We Have Learned

A. On your paper write the verb or verbs which you find in each sentence below.

1. David tended his father's sheep.
2. A lion stole a lamb.
3. David slew the lion.
4. Jesse called David.
5. He sent David to Saul.
6. David loved and trusted God.
7. We read and study the Bible.
8. Our class memorizes verses.
9. We learned the Twenty-third Psalm.
10. David wrote the words.
11. God cares for us.
12. He leads and protects us.
13. We love and honor God.
14. God never sleeps or slumbers.
15. Angels watch over us.

The Lord is my Shepherd, I shall not want.

B. Write a sentence to tell:

1. the sound a cat makes.
2. what your father does.
3. what a boy in your class does.
4. what you did last evening.
5. what children do in the snow.

C. When we sing songs we use verbs. Each set of words below is a line from a song. On your paper write the verb which will make the line from the song complete.

1. Jesus —— me
2. This I ——
3. For the Bible —— me so
4. When we —— with the Lord, in the light of His Word.
5. What a glory He —— on our way
6. While we —— His good will
7. He —— with us still
8. And with all who will —— and ——.
9. The wise man —— his house upon the rock.
10. I will —— you fishers of men.

D. Copy the five sentences below. Draw a line between the two parts of the sentence. Draw one line under each noun. Draw two lines under each verb.

1. Men and women sang.
2. Children followed.
3. Samuel listened and answered.
4. Jesus healed and taught.
5. The earth shook.

Review One

$\triangleright$ Oral Drill $\triangleright$

A. Answer these questions:

1. What is a noun?

2. What are some examples of common nouns?

3. What are some examples of proper nouns?

B. Find two nouns in each sentence below. Tell whether each noun names a **person, place,** or **thing.**

1. Mark read a book.

2. Father went to town.

3. That dog belongs to Uncle Bob.

4. Many fish live in the ocean.

5. Our grandparents went to Mexico.

6. The water splashed my brother.

7. Rice is grown in India.

8. Father prayed for peace.

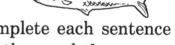

C. Use a **common** noun to complete each sentence below. You might have to add the word **the.**

1. —— sang.   4. We live in ——.

2. —— worked.   5. We visited ——.

3. —— prayed.   6. We go to ——.

D. Use a **proper** noun to complete each of the above sentences.

> Written Practice >

A. Find six proper nouns in the list below. Write the proper nouns correctly.

martha	woman	canada	ohio
house	mrs. weber	books	boys
jacob	king david	child	fish

B. Make three columns on your paper. Label the first column **Who,** the next one **What,** and the last one **Where.** Write each noun below in the correct column.

honesty	town	William	table
parents	Karen	country	India
animals	city	faith	girls

C. Write a complete sentence to answer each question below.

1. Who teaches school?
2. What grew in the garden?
3. Where are you?
4. Who is in first grade?
5. What does a cow eat?

Review Two

> Oral Drill >

A. What is a doing word?

B. Find the verbs in the sentences below.

1. Frogs croak.   6. Lee found a frog.
2. Mary sang.   7. Joy picked a daisy.
3. Sue waited.   8. Mother planted peas.
4. Tom smiled.   9. Bill ate a pear.
5. Dogs barked. 10. Ducks swim and fly.

C. Tell whether each sentence below needs a **noun** or a **verb** to be complete. Then complete each sentence correctly.

1. —— played.   6. John and Lee ——.
2. John ——.   7. —— read and write.
3. The girls ——.   8. Father and Mother ——.
4. —— spoke.   9. —— work and play.
5. Horses ——.   10. Swans and geese ——.

D. Use sentences to tell about what you see happening in your classroom right now. After you say each sentence, tell what verb you used.

Example: Jason reads a book.
             verb—reads

> Written Practice >

A. On your paper write whether the word in bold print in each sentence is a noun or a verb.

1. The **wind** blew.
2. I **found** a pencil.
3. Mother and I **worked**.
4. Judy petted the **puppy**.
5. **Open** the door please.
6. The grass was wet with **dew**.

B. Copy the four sentences below. Draw a line between the two parts of the sentence. Draw one line under each noun. Draw two lines under each verb.

1. The kittens slept.
2. Boys and girls played.
3. Uncle Bill waved and smiled.
4. David and Terry ran and hid.

C. Write three sentences to tell three things you did yesterday. Underline the verb in each sentence.

Example: I <u>went</u> to church.

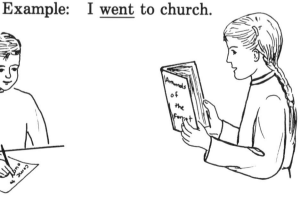

Extra Activity

Making a Sentence Wheel

Cut a large circle out of heavy paper. Draw a small circle in the center of the circle you cut out. Divide the large circle into eight even parts. Do the same thing on the other side of the large circle.

In the small circle on side one, write "God made." Find eight pictures of things that God made. Paste one in each of the outer parts of the circle. Underneath each picture write the noun which names what is shown.

In the small circle on side two, write "Children." Find eight pictures that show things that children do. Paste these in the outer part of the circle. Write the verb that each picture shows.

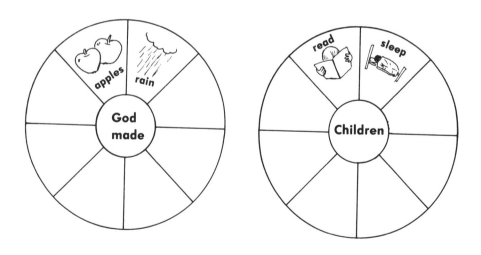

A Poem to Enjoy

Kind Words

Kind hearts are the gardens,
  Kind thoughts are the roots,
Kind words are the flowers,
  Kind deeds are the fruits.

Take care of the gardens,
  And keep them from weeds.
Fill, fill them with flowers,
  Kind words and kind deeds.
  —Longfellow

Discussing the poem:

1. What are some nouns in the first part of the poem?
2. What are some verbs in the second part of the poem?
3. How are our hearts like gardens?
4. What are some weeds that we have to keep out of our hearts?

Unit III

Pronouns: Another Building Block of English

"Pleasant words are as an honeycomb, sweet to the soul, and health to the bones."

Proverbs 16:24

1. Words That Stand for Nouns

When a person speaks about himself, he does not use his own name. He uses a word to take the place of his name. He says **I** or **me**.

Read the two paragraphs below.

"**I** went to school today," said Jacob. "The teacher asked **me** if **I** could read. She gave **me** a book."

"**Jacob** went to school today," said Jacob. "The teacher asked **Jacob** if **Jacob** could read. The teacher gave **Jacob** a book."

The first paragraph is written correctly. The words **I** and **me** are used properly. The second paragraph is not written correctly. In the second paragraph the words **I** and **me** are not used.

When you speak, you use the words **I** and **me** to talk about yourself. Sometimes when you write you must use **I** and **me**. You use **I** and **me** to take the place of your own name.

> For You to Do >

A. Think of some sentences to say about yourself. Use the words **I** and **me** in your sentences. Be ready to say your sentences in class.

B. Robert wrote the following sentences about himself. He used his own name. He did not use the words **I** and **me**. Rewrite the sentences, using either **I** or **me** to take the place of Robert's name. The first one is done for you.

1. **Robert** came home early.
   I came home early.
2. **Robert** was hungry.
3. Mother gave **Robert** an apple.
4. Then **Robert** went to the barn.
5. Father showed **Robert** the new calf.

> More Practice and Review >

A. What do you do after school? Do you have chores to do at home? Do you spend time reading? Write three sentences telling what you do after school. Use the word **I** in each sentence.

Example: After school **I** help Mother.

B. God has given us many good things. Write three sentences telling what God has given you. Use the word **me** in each sentence.

Example: God has given **me** good parents.

2. More About *I* and *Me*

When you speak and write about yourself, you do not always use your own name. You use the words **I** and **me** to take the place of your name. Your name is a **noun**. The words **I** and **me** are **pronouns**. **A pronoun is a word which takes the place of a noun.**

Susan is in second grade. Her teacher asked the class to write four sentences about being happy. Read the four sentences Susan wrote.

God wants **me** to be happy.
I am happy because God loves **me**.
I am happy when **I** obey.
Helping others makes **me** happy.

Did Susan use her own name when she wrote her sentences? No, she used the words **I** and **me** to take the place of her name. She used the **pronouns** **I** and **me** correctly.

When you write, remember to use the pronouns **I** and **me** correctly. Use these pronouns to take the place of your own name.

> Oral Drill >

Use **I** or **me** to complete each sentence below.

1. —— am in second grade.
2. Today —— am studying pronouns.
3. In school —— sing about Jesus.
4. Jesus loves ——.
5. —— read books about Jesus.
6. —— read the Bible.
7. The Bible teaches —— about God.
8. God sees —— all the time.
9. God gives —— many good things.
10. Sometimes —— am sick.
11. God takes care of ——.
12. —— should thank God for His care.
13. What does God want —— to do?
14. God wants —— to obey my parents.
15. —— must obey my teacher, too.

> For You to Do >

What happened last Sunday? Did you go to church? Who sat next to you? Did you go to somebody's house? Who played with you? Write six sentences telling what happened on Sunday. Use the pronouns **I** and **me** to take the place of your own name.

3. *You*

When we talk to someone about himself, we do not say his name. We use the word **you** to take the place of the name of the person with whom we are talking. We say, "Kevin, would **you** please help me?" We do not say, "Kevin, would **Kevin** please help me?"

The word **you** is a **pronoun**. The word **you** takes the place of a **noun**. **You** takes the place of the name of the person with whom we are talking.

Rachel wrote five sentences to another pupil in the second grade. Read the sentences that Rachel wrote.

You are a girl.
God gave **you** brown hair.
He gave **you** brown eyes.
You are taller than I am.
You are a good friend.

Rachel wrote to her friend Amy, but she did not use Amy's name. She used the pronoun **you** to take the place of Amy's name.

> For You to Do >

A. Write three sentences to another pupil in your class. Do not use the person's name. Use the pronoun **you** to take the place of his or her name. Be ready to read your sentences in class. See if the other pupils can guess to whom you wrote.

B. When we want to talk to someone, we should say the person's name and then say what we want to tell them. When we write what we have said to someone, we write the person's name first, and then write the rest of the sentence. We should put a comma after the person's name.

> Carl, you are a good friend.
> Janet, Mother made a dress for you.

Use the pronoun **you** to complete each sentence below. Then write each sentence correctly, putting a comma where it is needed. The first one is done for you.

1. James —— are eight years old.
   James, <u>you</u> are eight years old.
2. Clara I saw —— yesterday.
3. Paul would —— please help me?
4. Lois —— are Ruth's sister.
5. Keith did —— find the kittens?

4. The Pronoun *It*

A noun is a word which names a person, place, or thing. A table is a thing. The word table is a noun because it names a thing. Here are some more words which name things:

kitten   book   flower   sky   spider

When we talk, we often talk about things. We use a noun to name the thing we talk about. We can also use a pronoun when we talk about things. We can use the **pronoun it** to take the place of a **noun** which names a thing.

Read the pairs of sentences below. See how the **pronoun it** takes the place of a noun in the second sentence in each pair.

God made the world.
God made **it** in six days.

The Bible is God's Word.
It teaches us about God.

Never use the words **the, a,** or **an** with a pronoun. Do not use the words **this** or **that** with a pronoun.

Correct: **It** is broken.
Incorrect: **The it** is broken.

> **For You to Do** >

Use a noun to name each picture below. Write a sentence using the noun. Then write another sentence using the pronoun **it** to take the place of the noun.

Example: The **grass** is brown.
It needs more water.

1.   3.

2.   4.

> **More Practice and Review** >

Find the noun in each sentence below. Write the noun on your paper. Next to each noun write whether it names a **person** or a **thing**.

1. Samuel came quickly.
2. This melon is ripe.
3. The dog was barking.
4. A man came here.
5. That window is broken.
6. The girl sang cheerfully.
7. Brother John spoke seriously.
8. The hay is still wet.

5. Reviewing What We Have Learned

>Oral Drill>

Use a pronoun to take the place of the noun in bold print in each sentence. Say the sentence correctly.

1. Timothy, **Timothy** can run fast.
2. "**Janet** read that book," said Janet.
3. Who threw the **ball**?
4. Mark said, "Father told **Mark** to hurry home."
5. "**Samuel** saw a deer last evening," said Samuel.
6. Jacob, did **Jacob** ever see a deer?
7. Martha may use the **sled** now.
8. Lydia, would **Lydia** please help me?
9. James asked, "Did Father call **James**?"
10. Janet said, "**Janet** will help Mother."
11. "The **wasp** stung my hand," said Peter.
12. Lois, this book is for **Lois**.
13. Paul said, "God takes care of **Paul**."
14. Daniel, please put the **hammer** away.
15. Dorcas said, "Today **Dorcas** helped sweep."
16. "Uncle Noah wrote **Ray** a letter," said Ray.
17. Father found the **letter** in our mailbox.

18. "Uncle Noah wrote to **Joel**, too," said Joel.

19. Ruth, Aunt Mary wants to talk to **Ruth**.

20. "**Ruth** will come inside right now," said Ruth.

> Written Practice >

A. Think about a **thing** in your classroom. Write three sentences to tell about it. Be ready to read your sentences in class. See if the class can tell what you wrote about.

Example: **It** is smooth and flat.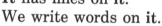
It has lines on it.
We write words on **it**.
What is **it**?

B. Think of the name of a friend. What do the two of you do together? Write three sentences telling what you do. Use your friend's name and the pronoun **I** together in each sentence.

Example: **Mark and I** walk to school.

C. We use pronouns every day. We say many sentences without even thinking about using pronouns. Below are some sentences we say to be courteous. Use a pronoun to complete each sentence. Write the sentences correctly.

1. Thank ——.

2. —— am sorry.

3. How do —— do?

4. Excuse ——, please.

6. *He* and *Him*

You learned that the words **I, me, you,** and **it** are pronouns. You can use the pronouns **I** and **me** to take the place of your own name. The pronoun **you** is used to take the place of the name of the person to whom you are speaking. The pronoun **it** is used to take the place of a noun which names a thing.

The words **he** and **him** are pronouns also. Read the sentence below. As you read the sentence, try to decide what noun the pronoun **he** is taking the place of.

Glen prayed before **he** ate.

In the sentence above, the pronoun **he** takes the place of the proper noun **Glenn.** We would not say:

Glenn prayed before **Glenn** ate.

We use the pronoun **he** to take the place of the noun **Glenn.**

Use the pronouns **he** and **him** when you are talking about a man or a boy. **He** and **him** are used to take the place of nouns which name a man or a boy.

Gerald came when Father called **him.**
Baby Peter smiled when **he** saw Mother.

> Oral Drill >

Find the pronoun in each sentence below. Name the noun which the pronoun stands for.

1. David was brave because he trusted God.
2. Moses listened when God spoke to him.
3. Noah did everything that he was told to do.
4. Cain sinned when he became angry.
5. When the boy was sick, Elijah prayed for him.
6. James obeyed Jesus and followed Him.
7. Peter wept after he had denied the Lord.
8. Jesus knew that Judas had betrayed Him.
9. Philip went where he was sent.
10. Philip spoke and the man listened to him.

> For You to Do >

A. Rewrite each sentence below. Use **he** or **him** to take the place of the noun in bold print.

1. Father asked **Carl** to weed the garden.
2. **Carl** obeyed Father.
3. **Steven** helped Sarah wash the dishes.
4. Sarah thanked **Steven** for his help.
5. Father visited **Mr. Green**.

B. Use each of the pronouns below in a sentence.

he   him   it   I   me

7. More About *He* and *Him*

You learned that the words **he** and **him** are pronouns. The pronouns **he** and **him** are used to take the place of a noun which names a man or a boy.

Paul preached the Gospel.
He visited many cities.

Paul spoke to the **jailer** in Philippi.
Paul told **him** about Jesus.

In the first pair of sentences above, the pronoun he takes the place of the noun **Paul**. In the second pair of sentences, the pronoun **him** is used to take the place of the noun **jailer.**

Do you remember what you learned about the pronoun **it**? The pronoun **it** is used to take the place of a noun which names a thing.

The **jar** broke when Eva dropped **it**.

Be careful to use pronouns correctly. Use **he** and **him** when talking about a man or a boy. Use **it** when talking about a thing.

Abraham built an altar.
He used stones to build it.

▷ Oral Drill ▷

Tell whether you would use the pronouns **he** and **him** or whether you would use the pronoun **it** to take the place of each noun.

brother	flower	minister
desk	hand	paper
Samuel	grandson	window
uncle	Timothy	deacon

▷ For You to Do ▷

A. Rewrite each sentence below, using the pronoun **he**, **him**, or **it** to take the place of each noun in bold print. Remember not to use the words **the**, **a**, and **an** with pronouns.

1. **Elijah** asked for some water.
2. The widow went to get the **water**.
3. She was going to get it for **Elijah**.
4. The **prophet** asked for bread, too.
5. The widow baked **bread** for **Elijah**.

B. Use the pronouns **he**, **him**, and **it** to help complete each sentence below. Write the sentences correctly. The first one is done for you.

1. <u>It</u> burned <u>him</u>.
2. —— read ——.
3. —— stung ——.
4. —— hurt ——.
5. —— opened ——.
6. —— saw ——.

8. *She* and *Her*

The pronoun family is very large. Today you will meet two more members of the pronoun family. Their names are **she** and **her**. When do you think we might use these two pronouns?

> **Mary** rejoiced when **she** met Jesus.
> Peter's **mother** was glad when Jesus healed **her**.

In the first sentence above, the pronoun **she** is used to take the place of the proper noun **Mary**. In the second sentence, the pronoun **her** is used to take the place of the noun **mother**. The nouns **Mary** and **mother** are used to refer to women. The pronouns **she** and **her** are used to refer to women also.

We use the pronouns **she** and **her** when we are talking about a woman or a girl.

> **Miriam** was Moses' sister.
> **She** had a brother named Aaron also.
>
> Jesus met a **woman** at the well.
> Jesus spoke to **her**.
>
> A **widow** helped Elijah.
> **She** gave him food to eat.
>
> Jairus had a **daughter**.
> Jesus healed **her**.

⟩ For You to Do ⟩

A. Rewrite each sentence below, using the pronoun **she** to take the place of the noun in bold print.

1. The **woman** believed Jesus.
2. Mary and **Martha** were sisters.
3. Where was **Hannah** praying?
4. The **girl** wanted to help Naaman.

B. Rewrite each sentence below, using the pronoun **her** to take the place of the noun in bold print.

1. Jesus spoke to a **woman**.
2. What did Jesus say to **Martha**?
3. God spoke to Aaron and **Miriam**.
4. Miriam watched the **princess** open the basket.

C. Decide whether you would use the pronouns **he** *and* **him** or **she** *and* **her**, or the pronoun **it** to take the place of each noun below. Write the correct pronouns on your paper. The first one is done for you.

1. son—**he, him**   4. niece   7. tractor
2. Aunt Ida   5. house   8. queen
3. grandfather   6. sister   9. Thomas

9. More Practice With *She* and *Her*

Read the two paragraphs below. Can you tell which paragraph is written correctly?

> Hannah did not have any children. Hannah prayed to God. The priest Eli saw Hannah praying. Eli told Hannah that God would give Hannah a son.

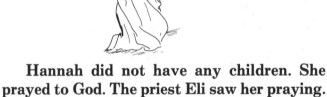

> Hannah did not have any children. She prayed to God. The priest Eli saw her praying. Eli told her that God would give her a son.

The first paragraph is not written correctly. In the first paragraph, the proper noun **Hannah** is used five times. The pronouns **she** and **her** are not used at all.

The second paragraph is written correctly. The first sentence uses the name **Hannah** to tell us whom the paragraph is about. The other sentences use the pronouns **she** and **her** to take the place of the noun **Hannah**.

Using pronouns helps give sentences variety. This means that we do not need to read the same words over and over again. When you write a paragraph, do not use the same noun over and over again. Use a pronoun to take the place of a noun.

> **For You to Do** >

Rewrite the paragraph below. Use either she or her to take the place of each noun in bold print.

Dorcas was a Christian. **Dorcas** helped many people. One time **Dorcas** became very sick and died. Peter prayed for **Dorcas**, and God made **Dorcas** alive again.

> **More Practice and Review** >

Think about a woman mentioned in the Bible. Write three sentences about the woman. Use the woman's name in the first sentence. Use the pronouns **she** and **her** in the other sentences.

10. Reviewing What We Have Learned

> Oral Drill

Use a pronoun to take the place of the noun in bold print in each sentence below. Read each sentence correctly.

1. "**Father** saw a deer today," said Father.
2. Paul, **Paul** should go help Mark now.
3. The **boy** carried the wood inside.
4. Where is **Mother**?
5. Father and **Mother** went to town.
6. Jason threw the ball, and Carl caught the **ball**.
7. Titus, please give this book back to **Gary**.
8. Esther ran to Mother and hugged **Mother**.
9. Sarah, Sister Anna sent a letter to **Sarah**.
10. Carla said, "Karen wrote **Carla** a letter."
11. Rhoda helped **Lois** wash the floor.
12. Where was **James** today?
13. Philip saw **James** at school.
14. June said, "Grace and **June** are sisters."
15. Richard asked, "Could Timothy help **Richard**?"
16. Uncle Ray found the **kitten** under the car.
17. **Mary** enjoyed visiting Ruth.
18. Ruth enjoyed visiting **Mary**.

> Written Practice >

A. Make your mind think and remember. Can you remember the eight pronouns which you have learned? Write each pronoun on your paper. Then use each pronoun correctly in a sentence.

B. On your paper write the pronoun which correctly completes each sentence below.

1. Kathy said (she, her) was hungry.
2. Mother gave (she, her) an apple.
3. Luke asked if (he, him) could have one.
4. (She, Her) washed another apple.
5. Mother gave (he, him) the apple.
6. The jar broke when Paul dropped (him, it).
7. The flower was pretty until (it, she) died.
8. Mother said that (she, her) needs some help.
9. Has anyone helped (she, her)?
10. Father spoke to (he, him).
11. Did (he, him) offer to help?
12. Martha washed a pear and gave (her, it) to Hope.
13. Where was (he, him) yesterday?
14. John saw (he, him) at school.
15. Joanna asked me to give the book to (she, her).

11. *We* and *Us*

You have been learning about pronouns that can take the place of a noun. The first pronouns that you met were **I** and **me**. You learned to use **I** and **me** to take the place of your own name when you are talking about yourself.

"Jay asked Roy to help Jay," said Jay.
"I asked Roy to help me," said Jay.

You use the pronouns **we** and **us** when you are talking about yourself, also. You use **we** and **us** when you are talking about yourself and someone else together.

Robert and I built a trap.
We used the trap to catch rabbits.

Mother asked Betty and me to help her.
She asked **us** to wash the floor.

Robert   I   Betty   me

we   us

> Oral Drill >

For each sentence below, use **we** or **us** to take the place of the words in bold print. Read each sentence correctly.

1. **Susie and I** visited Grandmother.
2. She said that she was glad to see **Susie and me.**
3. Uncle Bill waved to **Jesse and me.**
4. **Jesse and I** waved back to him.
5. **My brother and I** walk to school.
6. Sometimes Father gives **him and me** a ride.
7. **Jacob, Enos, and I** went fishing.
8. **My friends and I** like to sing.
9. Mother waited for **Naomi, Mary, and me.**
10. One day **my sister and I** were late.
11. Is there some work for **Daniel and me?**
12. Jesus loves **you and me.**
13. **She and I** washed the car for Father.
14. You can run faster than **Jacob and I** can.

> For You to Do >

Write eight sentences. Use each of the pronouns below twice.

I   we   me   us

12. *We* and *I, Us* and *Me*

John and I found a quarter.
We found a quarter.
Ruth spoke to Karen and me.
Ruth spoke to **us**.

Look at the first pair of sentences above. In the first sentence, the pronoun **I** is used. In the second sentence, the pronoun **we** is used. Whenever we use a pronoun to take the place of a noun or pronoun and the word **I**, we use the pronoun **we**.

She and I read *New Neighbors*.
We read *New Neighbors*.

Look at the second pair of sentences at the top of this page. In the first sentence in the pair, the pronoun **me** is used. In the second sentence, the pronoun **us** is used to take the place of the words **Karen and me**. Whenever we use a pronoun to take the place of a noun or pronoun and the word **me**, we use the pronoun **us**.

Did Father call you and me?
Did Father call **us**?

For You to Do

A. For each sentence below, decide whether you would use the pronoun **we** or **us** to take the place of the words in bold print. Write **we** or **us** on your paper.

1. One time **Luke and I** rode on a train.
2. Can **Martha and I** help you?
3. Sister Mary greeted **Grace and me**.
4. Father wants **you and me** to help milk.
5. May **John and I** help also?
6. Brother Paul waved to **Father and me**.
7. **He and I** were at the store.
8. Please call **Chris and me** when you are ready.
9. A letter came for **Terry and me**.
10. **My family and I** saw an elk yesterday.

B. Rewrite the following paragraph. Use **we** or **us** to take the place of the words in bold print.

> Jason and I built a wagon. First **Jason and I** found some wheels. Then Father gave **Jason and me** some boards. After **Jason and I** nailed the boards together, Father helped **Jason and me** put on the wheels and axles. He gave **Jason and me** some old pipe to use for the tongue.

13. *They* and *Them*

Are you ready to meet some more pronouns? **They** and **them** are two more words in the pronoun family. The words **they** and **them** help us talk about other people or things. We use **they** and **them** when we are talking about more than one person or thing.

> **The boys** are playing tag.
> **They** are playing freeze tag.

> **These books** are new.
> **They** were delivered yesterday.

> Did you meet **Lee and Ray**?
> Yes, I met **them** at school.

> Amos lost **his cap and gloves**.
> Jacob found **them** behind the stove.

▷ Oral Drill ▷

Use **they** or **them** to take the place of the words in bold print in each sentence below.

1. **The women** were sisters.
2. **James and John** were brothers.
3. Jesus blessed **the children**.
4. **The lepers** came to Jesus.
5. Jesus healed **the lepers**.
6. **The prison doors** were locked.
7. God opened **the doors**.
8. Dorcas helped **the widows**.

> **For You to Do** >

Use **they** or **them** to complete the sentences in each group below. Write the sentences correctly. Then use a complete sentence to answer each question.

1. a. —— give us our food and clothes.
   b. —— care for us.
   c. We love ——.
   d. We must obey ——.
   e. Who are ——?

2. a. We listen to —— in church.
   b. —— preach the Word of God.
   c. We must respect ——.
   d. —— are servants of God.
   e. Who are ——?

3. a. —— shine at night.
   b. God made —— on the fourth day.
   c. We cannot count ——.
   d. —— are very far away.
   e. What are ——?

14. More Practice With
They and *Them*

Look at the picture above. What do you see? Do the following sentences tell what you see?

> **Two calves are in the pen.**
> **The two calves are black and white.**
> **A boy is giving the calves milk.**

Look at the above sentences. The word **calves** is used in each sentence. We could write the last two sentences without using the word **calves**.

> Two calves are in the pen.
> **They** are black and white.
> A boy is giving **them** milk.

Look at the picture below. Read the sentences that tell about the picture. Notice how the pronouns **they** and **them** are used.

Some children are outside.
They are playing ball.
A dog is watching **them**.

Oral Drill

Say three sentences to tell about each picture below. Do not use the pronoun **they** or **them** in the first sentence about each picture. Use **they** and **them** in the second and third sentences.

For You to Do

Choose four of the pictures above. Write three sentences to go with each picture that you chose. Follow the rules given at the top of this page.

15. Reviewing What We Have Learned

> Written Practice >

A. 1. Make a list of the twelve pronouns which you have learned.

2. Write the sentence below seven times. Use a different pronoun to begin the sentence each time.

   —— fell.

3. Write the sentence below seven times. Use a different pronoun to end the sentence each time.

   God made ——.

4. Which two pronouns did you use for both number 2 and number 3 above?

5. Which pronouns did you use only for number 2?

6. Which pronouns did you use only for number 3?

B. Write the pronoun which correctly completes each sentence below.

1. (We, Us) learn about God's Word.

2. Our ministers teach (we, us).

3. Who teaches (they, them)?

4. (They, Them) study God's Word, too.

5. On Sunday (we, us) will go to church.

6. Will (they, them) be at church also?

⟩ Oral Drill ⟩

Use **we**, **us**, **they**, or **them** to take the place of the words in bold print in each sentence below.

1. Yesterday **Peter and I** went for a walk.
2. A dog barked at **Peter and me**.
3. **Our neighbors** own the dog.
4. **Peter and I** were not afraid.
5. In the woods, **Peter and I** saw some squirrels.
6. **The squirrels** were busy gathering nuts.
7. The squirrels did not see **Peter and me**.
8. We watched **the squirrels** for awhile.
9. Then **Peter and I** started home.
10. The hot sun had made **Peter and me** thirsty.
11. Where were **Rhoda and Esther**?
12. Mother said that **Rhoda and Esther** were in the barn.
13. Peter went to look for **Rhoda and Esther**.
14. **Mother and I** made some lemonade.
15. Mother and I waited for **Peter, Rhoda, and Esther**.
16. I gave **my brother and sisters** a drink.
17. The lemonade tasted very good to **my brother and sisters and me**.
18. **Rhoda, Esther, Peter, and I** thanked Mother.

16. One and More Than One

We say that a word which names only one single person or thing is **singular**. Here are some nouns which are singular:

book   child   house   goat   mouse

A word which names more than one is **plural**. Here are some plural nouns:

books   children   houses   goats   mice

Pronouns can be singular and plural also. A pronoun which names only one person or thing is singular. A pronoun which names more than one person or thing is plural.

I and **me** are singular pronouns. **I** and **me** are used to refer to one person.

How many does the pronoun **we** name? How many does the pronoun **us** name? **We** and **us** are used to name more than one person. **We** and **us** are plural pronouns.

You use the singular pronouns **I** and **me** to name yourself. You use the plural pronouns **we** and **us** to name yourself and someone else together.

I hoe the garden.   We shell the beans.

⊳ Oral Drill ⊳

Use **I**, **me**, **we**, or **us** to complete each sentence below.

1. The girls said, "—— should visit Sister Mae."
2. They said, "She will want —— to sing."
3. "—— should take song books," they said.
4. "Which one of —— will ring the bell?"
5. "—— will ring the bell," Karen offered.
6. "This is a surprise for ——," said Sister Mae.
7. "—— am very glad you came," she continued.
8. "Will you sing a song for ——?" she asked.
9. "—— will sing several songs," they said.
10. "Do you want to sing with ——?" they asked.
11. "—— will try to help sing," she smiled.
12. "What should —— sing first?" the girls wondered.

⊳ For You to Do ⊳

A. Write four sentences to tell about something you and your family did together. Use **we** in two of your sentences. Use **us** in two sentences.

B. Write four sentences to tell about something you did yesterday. Use **I** twice. Use **me** twice.

17. Using *You* for One or More

Some words can be either singular or plural. Some words can be used to name one person or thing, and can also be used to name more than one person or thing. Here are some nouns which can be used to name either one or more than one:

deer   sheep   hair   moose

The pronoun **you** can be used to name one person or more than one person. The pronoun **you** can be either singular or plural. Read the sentences below. In the first sentence, **you** names only one person. In the second sentence, **you** names more than one person.

> Jacob, **you** must come inside.
> Children, **you** should wash your hands.

When we want to talk to more than one person, we can still use the word **you**. We do not add an **s** to **you** to make **you** plural. We should never say **yous**.

> Boys, Father has some work for **you**.
> Girls, do **you** have any homework?
> Brian and Kevin, did **you** eat supper yet?

> ## For You to Do >

In each sentence below, decide whether **you** refers to one or more than one. If **you** refers to only one, write **singular** on your paper. If **you** refers to more than one, write **plural**.

1. You are my sister.
2. You are my friends.
3. Boys, I will give this job to you.
4. Mary, do you want this book?
5. You are our teacher.
6. You must both work cheerfully.
7. Girls, you may work together.
8. Were you ever here before, Paul?

> ## More Practice and Review >

Write the pronoun which correctly completes each sentence below.

1. Did (they, them) see the rainbow?
2. (Us, We) saw one yesterday.
3. Father told (us, we) to come outside.
4. (He, Him) was on the porch.
5. Mother was with (he, him).
6. (They, Them) pointed to the sky.
7. We looked where (they, them) pointed.
8. Father told (we, us) the story of the first rainbow.
9. Did (you, yous) ever hear the story?

18. *He, She, It,* **and** *They*

You learned to use the pronouns **he** and **him** when talking about one man or boy. You learned to use the pronouns **she** and **her** when talking about one woman or girl. You learned to use the pronoun **it** when talking about one thing.

The pronouns **he, him, she, her,** and **it** each name only one person or thing. **He, him, she, her,** and **it** are singular pronouns.

The pronouns **they** and **them** are used when you want to talk about more than one. **They** and **them** are plural pronouns. **They** and **them** can be used to talk about more than one person. **They** and **them** can be used to tell about more than one thing.

He reads.　　　She sews.　　　It wilted.

They sing.　　They write.　　They bloom.

Oral Drill

Tell whether you would use **he, she, it,** or **they** to take the place of each noun below.

nephew	princess	brethren	son
people	light	prophet	sun
paper	children	daughter	men
books	women	rabbit	ladies
maid	uncle	geese	Ruth

For You to Do

A. Write one sentence about each picture below. Use **he, she, it,** or **they** in each sentence.

1.

2.

3.

4.

5.

B. Write another sentence about each picture above. Use **him, her, it,** or **them** in each sentence.

19. Telling About More Than One

Read the following paragraph. Point to the pronouns as you read the sentences.

Father and Mother went to town together. They saw Mr. Green. Mr. Green waved to them. On the way home they found a kitten. They brought the kitten home.

What three words in the first sentence tell us who went to town? The words **Father and Mother** tell us who went to town.

Who saw Mr. Green? What one word is used to take the place of the three words **Father and Mother**? The pronoun **they** is used to take the place of the words **Father and Mother**.

Find the other two places where the word **they** is used. The word **they** takes the place of the words **Father and Mother** in the fourth and fifth sentences of the paragraph also.

Look at the third sentence. Whom did Mr. Green wave to? What word is used in the third sentence to take the place of the words **Father and Mother**?

We use the pronouns **they** and **them** when we want to tell about more than one person or thing. In the paragraph at the top of this page, the words **they** and **them** were used to tell about **Father and Mother**.

The sentence thought **They saw Mr. Green** could have been written as two sentences.

Father saw Mr. Green. **Mother** saw Mr. Green.

By combining these two sentence thoughts we could write:

Father and Mother saw Mr. Green.

We can use the pronoun **they** to take the place of the words **Father and Mother.**

They saw Mr. Green.

> **For You to Do** >

A. Rewrite each pair of sentences as one sentence. Use **they** or **them** to take the place of the words in bold print. The first one is done for you.

1. **He** saw me. **She** saw me.
   They saw me.

2. Mary called **him.** Mary called **her.**

3. Eva washed the **spoons.** Eva washed the **forks.**

4. **He** went home. **She** went home.

5. Did **he** walk? Did **she** walk?

B. Write four sentences about something you saw two or more people do together. Use **they** in two of your sentences. Use **them** in the other two sentences.

20. Reviewing What We Have Learned

> Oral Drill >

A. Each of the sentences below has two pronouns. One of the pronouns names only one person or thing. The other pronoun names more than one. Find the two pronouns in each sentence and tell which one is singular and which one is plural.

   1. He saw them yesterday.

   2. Boys, you and I should wash the car.

   3. Did you see us, Mary?

   4. We helped him shovel the snow.

   5. They gave me a book to read.

   6. They found it at school.

   7. She waited for us.

   8. Girls, did you thank her?

   9. We gave it to Mother.

  10. She gave them each an apple.

B. Use a pronoun to replace the words in bold print in each sentence. Read each sentence correctly.

   1. **Carla and I** found Skippy's puppies.

   2. **The puppies** are a week old now.

   3. Skippy barked at **Carla and me**.

   4. She did not want anyone to touch **the puppies**.

   5. **Jason and Isaac** are cousins.

6. **Mary and I** already set the table.

7. Who will help **her and me** peel the potatoes?

8. Robert will help peel **the potatoes.**

9. Do **Samuel and Paul** have a dog?

10. Jacob saw **the boys** petting a collie.

Written Practice

Under each picture below are two pronouns. Use these pronouns to help you write two sentences about each picture.

1.

we, us

3.

he, him

2.

they, them

4.

she, her

21. Using Pronouns Correctly

Read the sentence below. As you read it, try to decide whether you would use **I** or **me** to complete the sentence correctly.

> **Paul and —— washed the dishes.**

To decide whether to use **I** or **me** to complete the above sentence, think this way:

> Paul washed the dishes. *and*
> I washed the dishes.

Now put the two sentence thoughts together and say:

> **Paul and I** washed the dishes.

Here are some more sentences which you might combine the same way:

> Michael played ball. *and* I played ball.
> **Michael and I** played ball.
> Father called John. *and* Father called me.
> Father called **John and me.**
> Peter helped Jason. *and* Peter helped me.
> Peter helped **Jason and me.**

▷ Oral Drill ▷

Use **I** or **me** to complete each sentence below.

1. Jason and —— helped Brother Ben.
2. Kathy and —— baked cookies.
3. Baby Paul watched Kathy and ——.
4. God cares for you and ——.
5. Today Enos and —— must walk home.
6. Father cannot come for Enos and ——.
7. My brothers and —— like to sing.
8. Sometimes Terry and —— sing in the barn.

▷ For You to Do ▷

A. Use **I** or **me** to complete the second sentence in each pair below. Then write another sentence by putting the two sentence thoughts together.

1. a. Paul went home.   b. _I_ went home.

   Paul and I went home.

2. a. Joy helped Mother.   b. —— helped Mother.
3. a. God made you.   b. God made ——.
4. a. Bob spoke to Ray.   b. Bob spoke to ——.
5. a. Ben saw the calf.   b. —— saw the calf.
6. a. Joan called Ruth.   b. Joan called ——.

B. Write the answers for the **Oral Drill** at the top of this page. You need to write only **I** or **me**.

22. More Practice With *I* and *Me*

God's Word is wonderful. In His Word He tells us how to do what is right. He tells us how to treat other people. Here is one Bible verse which tells us how to treat others:

> **"Be kindly affectioned one to another with brotherly love; in honour preferring one another." (Romans 12:10)**

The verse tells us to *prefer* one another. This means that we should think about someone else before we think about ourselves. It means that we should treat others with courtesy and respect.

We show this courtesy in many ways. One way we show it is when we are walking with someone. When we come to a door, we open the door and step back. We let the other person go through the door first.

We can show this courtesy when we speak and write, too. Yes, even our speech can show whether we are "preferring one another." When we speak or write about someone else and ourselves, we should always say the other person's name first. We should say **I** or **me** last.

MOTHER   I

Say: **Mother** and **I** baked a cake.
Father spoke to **Robert** and **me**.

Let the name of the other person go first. Then let **I** or **me** follow.

ROBERT   ME

> **For You to Do**

Copy each sentence below. Put **I** or **me** in each blank. In your mind, break the sentence into two parts to help you decide which pronoun to use.

1. Janet and —— fed the chickens.
2. The teacher spoke to Mark and ——.
3. May Sarah and —— have some cookies?
4. Who gave the book to Kevin and ——?
5. Joseph and —— must go home.
6. The children called my sister and ——.

> **More Practice and Review**

Write the pronoun which correctly completes each sentence below.

1. Mary and (me, I) walked home.
2. Mother read a story to (us, we).
3. (She, Her) read about Elisha.
4. A widow went to (he, him).
5. The prophet spoke to (she, her).
6. Mother handed the book to Mary and (I, me).

23. Using Nouns and Pronouns

What is the correct way to complete the sentence below? Would you use **he** or **him** to complete the sentence?

Philip and —— painted the porch.

To help you know which pronoun to use, say:

Philip painted the porch. *and*
He painted the porch.

Now join your two sentence thoughts and say:

Philip and he painted the porch.

Here are some more sentences which can be completed the same way. Choose he or him for the first sentence and she or her for the second and third sentences.

Father called May and ——.
Father called May. *and* Father called **him**.
Father called **May and him**.

Mother and —— shelled peas.
Mother shelled peas. *and* **She** shelled peas.
Mother and she shelled peas.

The bees stung Jay and ——.
The bees stung Jay. *and* The bees stung **her**.
The bees stung **Jay and her**.

Think carefully when you use pronouns. If you are using a noun and a pronoun together, take time to find the correct pronoun to use.

> Oral Drill >

Choose the correct pronoun to use to complete each sentence below.

1. Father and (he, him) cut the wood.
2. Eunice and (she, her) stacked the wood.
3. David waved to Paul and (he, him).
4. Mother visited Martha and (she, her).
5. Please ask Robert and (he, him) to come.
6. Did you see Priscilla and (she, her)?
7. Ruth and (she, her) made supper.
8. Where did William and (he, him) go?
9. (She, Her) and (I, me) are ready.
10. Martha saw (he, him) and (I, me).

> For You to Do >

A. Combine the sentences in each pair to make one sentence. Write the new sentence correctly.

1. Paul called John.   Paul called him.
2. Peter picked apples.   She picked apples.
3. James can read.   He can read.
4. She left early.   I left early.
5. He waited.   I waited.

B. Write the answers for the **Oral Drill**.

24. More Practice With Nouns and Pronouns

Ruth saw Timothy.
Timothy saw Ruth.

Look at the two sentences above. The noun **Ruth** is used in both sentences. But in each sentence the noun **Ruth** has a different job to do. In the first sentence **Ruth** tells us **who** saw Timothy. In the second sentence **Ruth** tells us **whom** Timothy saw.

What pronoun could we use to take the place of the noun **Ruth** in the first sentence above?

She saw Timothy.

The pronoun **she** can take the place of the noun **Ruth** in the first sentence. Can **she** take the place of **Ruth** in the second sentence? No, we would not say: Timothy saw **she**. We must use the pronoun **her**.

Timothy saw **her**.

When we use pronouns, we must be careful to use each one correctly. We must be certain that we use each pronoun to do the job that it is made to do.

What pronoun can take the place of the noun **Timothy** in the first sentence at the top of the previous page? What pronoun can take the place of **Timothy** in the second sentence?

> Ruth saw **him**.
> **He** saw Ruth.

> For You to Do >

A. Rewrite each pair of sentences. Use a pronoun to take the place of the words in bold print.

1. **Kathy** helped Martha.
   Martha helped **Kathy**.
2. **The boys** liked the dog.
   The dog liked **the boys**.
3. Did **James** find Paul?
   Did Paul find **James**?

4. **Bill and I** waited for Kevin.
   Kevin waited for **Bill and me**.

B. Read the two questions below. Look at the pronouns at the bottom of the page. Which pronouns could you use to complete the answer to the first question? Which pronouns would complete the answer to the second question? Write each answer five times. Use a different pronoun each time.

1. *Who* did it?   2. *Whom* did it hurt?
   —— did it.   It hurt ——.

   I   me   he   him   she   her   we   us   they   them

25. Reviewing What We Have Learned

▷ Oral Drill ▷

Choose the correct pronoun to complete each sentence below. Read each sentence correctly.

1. Paula and (I, me) baked a cake.
2. Mother and (she, her) frosted it.
3. I watched Mother and (she, her).
4. Did you meet Brian and (he, him)?
5. We saw the girls and (they, them) today.
6. What did Brian and (he, him) do?
7. They waved to Father and (I, me).
8. Kenneth and (I, me) helped Father and Mother.
9. Father and (she, her) thanked us.
10. Did you help Father and (she, her)?
11. We helped Mother and (he, him).
12. Mother and (he, him) wanted to shell nuts.
13. The dog barked at Janet and (I, me).
14. Yesterday Sally and (I, me) picked pears.
15. The girls and (she, her) made a quilt.
16. The boys and (he, him) cleaned the barn.
17. Aunt Esther helped the girls and (she, her).
18. A package came for Philip and (I, me).
19. Did a letter come for Rhoda and (he, him)?
20. Rhoda and (he, him) received a post card.

> **Written Practice** >

A. Use the two pronouns following each sentence to fill in the blanks. Be careful to use each pronoun correctly.

1. —— called ——.   **she, me**
2. —— heard ——.   **them, we**
3. —— greeted ——.   **her, I**
4. —— found ——.   **he, us**
5. —— helped ——.   **him, they**

B. Use each phrase below to help you build a sentence. Check your sentences to be certain that the pronouns are used correctly.

1. Martha and I
2. Father and me
3. Aunt Mary and her
4. The boys and him
5. Karen and she
6. Kevin and he

Review One

⟩ Oral Drill ⟩

Use this list of pronouns to help you do the following exercises:

I   you   he   she   we   they
me   it   him   her   us   them

A. Tell which pronouns you would use:

1. when you are talking about yourself.
2. to take the place of the name of the person to whom you are talking.
3. when you are talking about a man or a boy.
4. when you are talking about a woman or a girl.
5. when you are talking about a thing.
6. when you are talking about yourself and someone else together.
7. when you are talking about more than one person or thing.

B. Answer these questions:

1. Which pronoun is always written with a capital letter?
2. Which pronouns are **singular**?
3. Which pronouns are **plural**?
4. Which pronoun can be either singular or plural?

> Written Practice >

A. On your paper write whether you would use: **he** *and* **him**, **she** *and* **her**, **it**, or **they** *and* **them** to take the place of each noun below.

1. Mark   5. niece   9. dishes
2. Sarah   6. parents   10. blanket
3. table   7. grandson   11. mother
4. geese   8. house   12. brother

B. Write the pronoun you would use to take the place of the noun in bold print in each of the sentences below.

1. Karen, **Karen** may have an apple.
2. John said, "**John** read the story."
3. Glenn said, "Please pass **Glenn** the bread."
4. **Susan** is Carl's sister.
5. Jacob helped **Mother** in the garden.
6. **Jacob** picked the beans.
7. The **boys** are helping Father.
8. Who caught the **ball**?
9. Brian threw it to **Andy**.
10. Lois found the **cows** by the creek.

C. Use each of these pronouns in a sentence:

I   me   we   us

Review Two

Oral Drill

A. Use the phrases below correctly in sentences.

1. Ruth and I
2. Carol and me
3. Jason and he
4. Susan and him
5. Lois and she
6. Steven and her

B. Use the correct pronoun to complete each sentence below.

1. Father gave it to Carl and (I, me).
2. (They, Them) have a brown dog.
3. (She, Her) folded the towels.
4. Chris waited for (he, him).
5. Please read a story to (we, us).
6. Mother and (I, me) made some cookies.
7. Robert made a stool for (she, her).
8. Please return these books to (they, them).
9. Ben and (he, him) are in the third grade.
10. (We, Us) gathered the eggs.
11. Bob mowed the lawn, and I raked (her, it).
12. Baby Sue was sleepy, so Mother rocked (her, it).
13. We saw Father and waved to (him, it).
14. Joy swept the floor, and then she washed (him, it).
15. Peter and (I, me) rode the pony.

> **Written Practice** >

A. Write whether you would use **we, us, they,** or **them** to take the place of the words in bold print in each sentence below.

1. **Kathy and I** did the dishes.
2. **Timothy and Seth** shoveled the snow.
3. Father saw **Uncle Paul and Aunt Mary**.
4. Brother Lee waved to **Howard and me**.
5. **Sister Lois and he** were at church Sunday.
6. Mother spoke to **Martha and her**.
7. Grandmother sent a letter to **Eva and me**.
8. **My father and I** milked the goats.

B. Under each picture below are two pronouns. Use the pronouns to help you write two sentences about each picture.

1. she, her

2. he, him

3. they, them

Extra Activity

Making A Card

Do you know somebody who is sick? Do you know somebody who cannot always go to church? Wouldn't it be kind to make a card for this person?

Use a sheet of plain paper. Fold the paper in half. On the outside of the card, copy neatly Psalm 121:2. Paste some pretty pictures or seals around this verse.

On the inside, copy the poem from the opposite page. Perhaps you will want to add a message of your own also.

A Poem to Enjoy

Love

Love will make us well-behaved
In each word and deed;
It will think of others first—
To their needs give heed.

Love will keep us sweet and kind
When we're treated ill;
Praising God for doing well
What is His good will.

Discussing the poem:

1. What are some things the poem says love will do?

2. How do you think love will make us well-behaved?

3. How do you think love will keep us sweet and kind?

4. Can you think of any other things that love might do?

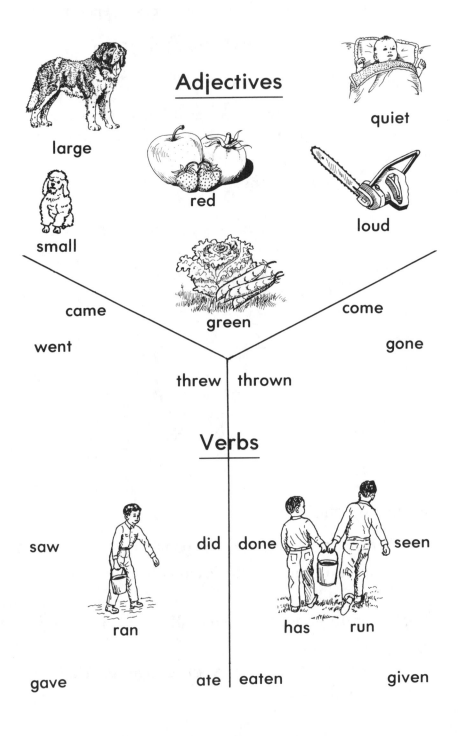

Adjectives

large

quiet

red

small

loud

green

came

come

went

gone

threw | thrown

Verbs

saw

did | done

seen

ran

has

run

gave

ate | eaten

given

Unit IV

Meeting More Building Blocks of English

"A word fitly spoken is like apples of gold in pictures of silver."

Proverbs 25:11

1. Telling About Nouns

A noun is a word which names a person, place, or thing. Here are some nouns:

> king   village   city   apple   **frog**

We can use verbs to help tell about nouns.

> The frog **croaks**.
> The frog **jumped**.

The words **croaks** and **jumped** are verbs. **Jumped** and **croaks** tell us what the frog does or did.

Other words tell about nouns also.

 The frog is **green**.
The **green** frog jumped.

Green tells us what color the frog is. We can use other words to tell about the frog also.

 The frog is **old**.
The **old** frog jumped.

The frog is **big**.
The **big** frog jumped.

Can you think of some more words to describe the frog? Think of some more words to complete these sentences:

> The frog is ——.
> The —— frog jumped.

⊃ Oral Drill ⊃

Choose a word to fill in the blanks in each pair of sentences below.

1. The boy is ——.
   The —— boy smiled.

2. The dog is ——.
   The —— dog barked.

3. The bees are ——.
   The —— bees buzzed.

4. The snow is ——.
   The —— snow melted.

5. The horse is ——.
   The —— horse ran.

6. The coat is ——.
   The —— coat tore.

7. The duck is ——.
   The —— duck swam.

8. The girl is ——.
   The —— girl sang.

⊃ For You to Do ⊃

Use a word from the list to complete each sentence. Write each sentence correctly. Draw a circle around each noun.

soft	empty	sticky	black	hot
loud	happy	sweet	green	tall

1. The noise is ——.
2. The grass is ——.
3. The glue is ——.
4. The pillow is ——.
5. The cake is ——.

6. The cup is——.
7. The tree is ——.
8. The boys are ——.
9. The calf is ——.
10. The fire is ——.

2. Describing Nouns

brown   happy   little   tired   cold

Look at the words at the top of this page. Each of the words helps to tell more about a person, place, or thing. Each of the words can be used to describe a noun.

Use each of the words at the top of this page to fill in the blanks in these sentences:

The puppy is ——.
The —— puppy barked.

Words such as **brown, happy,** and **little** are called **adjectives.** We use adjectives with nouns to tell about persons, places, or things.

Read the phrases below. The words in bold print are adjectives. Each adjective helps tell about the person or thing which the noun names.

a **tiny** baby   a **busy** mother   a **dead** tree

a **yellow** flower   **white** snow   a **cloudy** sky

> **For You to Do** >

A. On your paper copy the phrases below. Next to each phrase write the letter of the picture which goes with each phrase.

1. a broken chair
2. a soft chair
3. a rocking chair
4. a high chair
5. a little chair
6. a striped chair

A   B   C   D   E   F

B. Can you put together the sentence puzzle below? Choose an adjective from the pieces at the left to fill in the first blank in each sentence. Choose a verb from the pieces at the right to fill in the second blank. Write each sentence correctly.

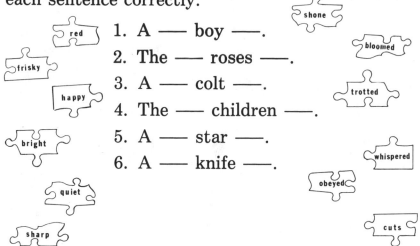

red · frisky · happy · bright · quiet · sharp

shone · bloomed · trotted · whispered · obeyed · cuts

1. A — boy —.
2. The — roses —.
3. A — colt —.
4. The — children —.
5. A — star —.
6. A — knife —.

3. What Color Is It?

God has made our eyes in a wonderful way. He has made our eyes so that we can see the many colorful things which He has made. We can see **white** lilies and **red** roses. We can see the clear **blue** sky or the large **gray** rain clouds.

Words which tell **what color** are one type of adjective. We use words which tell what color with nouns to help tell about what we see.

  Susan saw a **yellow** flower.
Joann saw a **pink** flower.
Paul saw a **purple** flower.

God has made it possible for us to see colors. When we write about things, we can use adjectives to tell what color each thing is. Then other people can picture the many colorful things which God has made, too.

> For You to Do >

A. Look at the rainbow on the previous page. Write the names of the six colors which God put in the rainbow. Next to each color, write a noun which the color might describe.

Example: yellow—butterfly

B. Here are the names of four colors which are not found in the rainbow:

black   gray   white   brown

Write these four colors on your paper. Next to each color write a noun which the color might describe.

C. Copy the list of nouns below. After each noun, write a color which might describe that noun.

Example: coal—black

1. clouds
2. sky
3. grapes
4. pumpkins
5. tomatoes

6. dandelions
7. horse
8. kitten
9. wood
10. leaves

4. Answering Questions With Adjectives

Adjectives are used to help tell about nouns. Some adjectives can answer the question **what color.**

What color is a bird?
A cardinal is **red.**
A flamingo is **pink.**
A raven is **black.**

What size and **what kind** are two more questions which adjectives can answer. Here are some adjectives which can answer **what size:**

| small | huge | tiny | short | thin |
| big | wide | high | narrow | little |

What size is the tree?
The tree is **tall.**
What size is an elephant?
An elephant is **large.**

Here are some adjectives which can answer the question **what kind:**

| polite | pretty | noisy | busy | soft |
| helpful | gentle | easy | new | wild |

What kind of child smiles?
A **happy** child smiles.
What kind of man has wisdom?
A **wise** man has wisdom.

> Oral Drill >

| daisy | pony | chair | blanket |
| snake | cake | dress | book |

For each noun in the box above:

1. Use an adjective to tell **what color.**

2. Use an adjective to tell **what size.**

3. Use an adjective to tell **what kind.**

> For You to Do >

A. Copy the adjective used in each phrase below. After each adjective, write whether it tells **what color** or **what size.**

1. little berries   5. gray clouds
2. long fingers   6. high buildings
3. white cotton   7. silver coins
4. wide ocean   8. blond hair

B. Copy each noun listed below. After each noun write two adjectives to tell more about the noun.

children   coat   city   house   apple

5. Reviewing What We Have Learned

◁ Oral Drill ▷

Use an adjective to complete the sentences in each pair below.

1. The robin is ——.
   The —— robin flew.
2. The ice is ——.
   The —— ice melted.
3. The children are ——.
   The —— children laughed.
4. The women are ——.
   The —— women sang.
5. The pony is ——.
   The —— pony gallops.

6. The boy is ——.
   The —— boy waited.
7. The girl is ——.
   The —— girl smiled.
8. The flower was ——.
   The —— flower wilted.
9. The milk was ——.
   The —— milk spoiled.
10. The wind was ——.
    The —— wind blew.
11. The men were ——.
    The —— men worked.

12. The stars are ——.

The —— stars twinkle.

> **Written Practice** >

A. Look at the picture below. Use nouns to name five things you see. Next to each noun, write two adjectives which would tell about what is being named.

B. Use each of the phrases below in a sentence. The words in bold print are adjectives.

1. an **orange** butterfly

2. a **hurt** puppy

3. the **hungry** kitten

4. a **helpful** boy

5. the **smallest** cookie

6. Working With Adjectives

Mary said, "Ellen has a calf."
Amy said, "Ellen has a gentle, brown calf."

Read what Mary and Amy said. Which girl told us more about Ellen's calf? Mary only told us that Ellen has a calf. When we read Mary's sentence, we do not know what kind of calf Ellen had.

Amy told us more about Ellen's calf. Amy told us **what color** Ellen's calf is. She told us that it is a **brown** calf. She also told us **what kind** of calf it is. She told us that it is a **gentle** calf.

The words **gentle** and **brown** are adjectives. Amy used adjectives to help tell about Ellen's calf. The adjectives **gentle** and **brown** help us see Ellen's calf in our mind.

Read each sentence below. Notice how the words in bold print suggest a clearer picture in your mind.

Uncle Ray rides a horse.
Uncle Ray rides a **big, black** horse.

The squirrels gathered nuts.
The **busy, gray** squirrels gathered nuts.

⟩ Oral Drill ⟩

Find two adjectives in each sentence below.

1. They filled the tall, gray silo.
2. The happy, little baby smiled.

3. The small, brown bird sang.

4. Carl has a new, blue coat.

5. The pretty, pink flowers died.

6. They live in a large, white house.

7. Mother has an old, wooden spoon.

8. We saw a harmless, green snake.

9. The sweet, green peas ripened.

10. A cold, damp wind blew.

> For You to Do >

Choose an adjective from the list to complete each sentence below. Write each sentence correctly. You will not need to use all the adjectives.

1. The —— dog barked.	stale	cloudy
2. We saw a —— bird.	blue	joyful
3. The bread is ——.	large	friendly
4. A —— man helped me.	tired	yellow
5. The sky is ——.	kind	strange
6. The —— boy slept.	fresh	little
7. The —— boys sang.	wise	happy
8. The —— man prayed.	gray	faithful

7. Describing What We See

Some adjectives help us tell about things we see. Adjectives which tell **what color** help us describe what we see.

> I saw a **brown** horse.
> We can see the **blue** sky.

Adjectives which tell **what size** can also be used to describe what we see.

James saw a **large** airplane.
Will the cat see the **little** bird?

Other adjectives can tell **what shape** something is. We can use adjectives which tell **what shape** to help us describe what we see.

> Mary saw the **round** cake.
> Did Mother see the **bent** spoon?

Look at this page. Use your eyes carefully. What color is the paper? What shape is the page? What size is the book?

> The paper is **white**.
> The page is **rectangular**.
> The book is **thin**.

Oral Drill

Each noun below names something you can see in your classroom. For each noun, use two adjectives to help describe what you see.

1. chalk board   4. book   7. clock
2. pencil   5. floor 8. desk
3. chair   6. walls 9. ruler

For You to Do

A. For each picture below, write a noun to name what you see. Then choose two adjectives from the list which could describe what you see. Write the adjectives after each noun.

1.   2.   3.

4.   5.

flowered	spotted	round	tall	empty
striped	little	shaggy	red	green

B. Think about something you saw on your way to school. Write a sentence telling about what you saw. Use at least one adjective in your sentence.

8. Describing What We Hear

God made us in a marvelous way. He gave us eyes to see many wonderful things. He gave us ears to hear many different sounds.

Read each noun below. As you read each word, try to think how the thing which is named sounds.

siren   bell   chainsaw   shout   whisper

We can use adjectives to describe the many sounds which we hear. Here are some ways which we might describe a siren:

a loud siren   a shrill siren   a noisy siren

Read the phrases below. The words in bold print are adjectives. Each adjective is used to help describe how something sounds.

a **soft** whisper   the **booming** thunder
a **high** voice   a **quiet** song
a **sad** cry   a **tinkling** bell

Whenever we use an adjective to describe a sound, we should choose an adjective which will describe well the sound that we heard. We should choose an adjective which will help somebody else know exactly what we heard.

> Oral Drill >

A. Take turns in class reading this sentence:

I am in second grade.

Read the sentence:

in your **normal** voice   in a **high** voice
in a **soft** whisper   in a **deep** voice

B. Find the adjective in each phrase below. Tell whether the adjective **helps you see** or **helps you hear** what is being described.

1. bright lightning
2. loud thunder
3. a red bird
4. a singing bird
5. a gruff voice
6. a wide river
7. a squeaky door
8. a large door
9. a low window
10. a low whisper

> For You to Do >

A. Choose five of the phrases from part B of the Oral Drill. Use each phrase that you chose in a sentence.

B. Copy the nouns given below. After each noun, write the adjectives that could describe it. You may use each adjective more than once.

Nouns: thunder   whisper   voice   shout
Adjectives: loud   shrill   quiet
            soft   squeaky   noisy

9. Using Adjectives

Sister Anne asked each pupil in her class to describe his or her house.

> Kathy said, "We live in a large, **red**, **brick** house."
> Mark said, "We live in an **old**, **stone** house."
> Alice said, "We live in a **little**, **gray** house."
> Terry said, "We live in a **new**, **white** house."

Each child used adjectives to describe his or her house. The adjectives tell how each house is different. Each child's sentence helps you picture a different house.

Read the pairs of phrases below. In each pair of phrases, the noun is the same, but the adjectives are different. The adjectives help you see different pictures in your mind.

a **big**, **white** dog
a **little**, **brown** dog

a **tiny**, **pink** flower
a **large**, **purple** flower

an **empty** cup
a **full** cup

> ## For You to Do

A. Next to each number, write the name of the fruit which is being described. Use the list to help you.

1. a wrinkled, brown fruit   **banana**

2. a round, orange fruit   **apple**

3. a round, yellow fruit   **grape**

4. a long, yellow fruit   **orange**

5. a smooth, red fruit   **raisin**

6. a round, purple fruit   **apricot**

7. a fuzzy, orange fruit   **grapefruit**

B. Copy each phrase below. Underline the noun. Circle the adjective. Then rewrite each phrase, using a different adjective to make a different picture in your mind.

Example: a (tall) tree
    a dead tree

1. a new dress

2. brown hair

3. a dirt road

4. a happy face

C. Write one sentence to describe your house. Then write another sentence to describe the house of one of your friends.

10. Reviewing What We Have Learned

Oral Drill

A. Find two adjectives in each sentence below.

1. The little, black pony neighed.
2. The children were obedient and happy.
3. The big red rooster crowed.
4. The loud thunder and heavy rain woke us.
5. An elephant is large and gray.
6. The boys played in the clean, white snow.
7. Grandmother gave us the sticky, sweet candy.
8. The hot soup was delicious.
9. The busy mother sang a cheerful song.
10. Bill is tall, and Samuel is short.

B. Use an adjective to complete each sentence below.

1. The —— girl sang as she worked.
2. The —— tree had lost its leaves.
3. The —— water tasted good.
4. The —— birds pecked at the seeds.
5. —— clouds filled the sky.
6. The —— man helped the stranger.
7. A giraffe is very ——.
8. One of our cows is ——.
9. The weather in winter is ——.
10. —— flowers bloom in the spring.

> Written Practice >

A. Write a complete sentence to answer each question below. Use the list of adjectives to help you. The first one is done for you.

1. What kind of child smiles?
   A happy child smiles.
2. What size is a sparrow?
3. What color is a carrot?
4. What kind of thunder did Tom hear?
5. What shape is an orange?
6. What kind of tree has acorns?

orange   oak   round   small   happy   loud

B. Find the adjectives in the phrases below. Write the adjectives on your paper.

1. the quiet children
2. a spotted calf
3. bright sunlight
4. a cold wind
5. sharp stones
6. smooth sheets
7. fuzzy blankets
8. high buildings
9. a shrill whistle
10. soft fur
11. a pleasant day
12. a clear sky
13. the sick baby
14. new boots

11. Building Better Sentences

The wind blew.
The wind was cold.

Read the two sentences at the top of this page. Both sentences tell about the same wind. Can you find the verb in the first sentence? The verb is **blew**. The verb **blew** tells us what the wind did.

Look at the second sentence. Can you find the adjective which describes the wind? The adjective **cold** is used to describe the wind.

From the two sentences, we learn that the wind blew and that it was cold. Do you know how we could use one sentence to say the same thing? Let us take the adjective out of the second sentence and put it in the first sentence. Then we can say:

The **cold** wind blew.

Here are some more sentences which we could combine the same way:

The hen cackled.
The hen was **red**.   The **red** hen cackled.

The boy slept.
The boy was **tired**.   The **tired** boy slept.

▷ Oral Drill ▷

Combine the two sentences in each pair to make one sentence which says the same thing.

1. The kitten cried. The kitten was lost.
2. The man spoke. The man was kind.
3. The sun shone. The sun was hot.
4. The dress tore. The dress was new.
5. The knife cut her. The knife was sharp.
6. The boys sang. The boys were happy.
7. The dog panted. The dog was thirsty.
8. The girls played. The girls were quiet.
9. The pony trotted. The pony was brown.
10. The stars twinkled. The stars were bright.

> **For You to Do** >

Combine the two sentences in each pair to make one sentence which says the same thing. Write the new sentence correctly.

1. The men worked. The men were busy.
2. The sun rose. The sun was red.
3. The dog limped. The dog was hurt.
4. The car stopped. The car was old.
5. The bear growled. The bear was black.
6. The fox ran. The fox was gray.

12. How Many?

You learned that adjectives are used to tell about nouns. Some adjectives answer the question **what color**. Some adjectives answer the question **what size** or **what kind**.

Number words are used to tell about nouns, also. Number words are used to answer the question **how many. How many** lepers did Jesus heal? **How many** lepers thanked Jesus?

> Jesus healed **ten** lepers.
> **One** leper thanked Jesus.

The number words **ten** and **one** tell **how many** in each sentence above. The word **ten** tells exactly how many lepers Jesus healed. The word **one** tells exactly how many lepers thanked Jesus.

Number words can be used to tell exactly how many. When we do not know exactly how many, we can say **some, several,** or **many**. The words **some, several,** and **many** are used to tell about the nouns in bold print in these sentences:

> Some **people** have blue eyes.
> Several **boys** helped paint the house.
> Many **people** live in North America.

> For You to Do >

A. On your paper, write the word which tells:

1. how many children are in your classroom
2. how many teachers are in your school
3. how many brothers and sisters you have
4. how many trees God made
5. how many rooms are in your house

B. Use a word which tells **how many** to complete each sentence below. Write each sentence correctly.

1. — animals live in the woods.
2. Father saw — deer yesterday.
3. — rabbits have been seen by Timothy.

C. Look at each picture below. Write a sentence about each picture. Use a number word to tell exactly how many.

Example:

One window is open.

1.

2.

3.

13. Saying What We Mean

Susan went to the store for Mother. The clerk asked Susan what she needed.

Susan said, "I am looking for bowls."

The clerk did not know exactly what Susan meant.

"What kind of bowls?" the clerk asked.

"Mixing bowls," Susan said.

"What size?" the clerk wondered.

"Large mixing bowls," Susan answered.

"How many do you need?" the clerk asked.

"Three," Susan said.

Now the clerk knew exactly what Susan meant.

Susan should have told the clerk, "I am looking for three large mixing bowls." Then the clerk would not have wondered **what kind**, **what size**, or **how many**. The clerk would have known right away what Susan meant.

When we build sentences, we must choose our words carefully. We must choose nouns, pronouns, and verbs which help us say what we mean. We must also choose adjectives and number words to help us say what we mean. When you speak and write, choose adjectives and number words which will help you say exactly what you mean.

> Oral Drill >

Take turns in class using adjectives to complete the sentences below. See how many different words you can use.

1. Father bought a —, — horse.
2. Mother bought some —, — fabric.
3. Uncle Ben bought a —, — tractor.
4. Grace found a —, — kitten.
5. Tim saw a —, — bird.

> For You to Do >

Choose words from the list to complete each sentence below. You will not need to use all the words. Write each sentence correctly.

1. Jane saw —, — houses.
2. Paul found a —, — puppy.
3. Chris has a —, — wagon.
4. Father gave Lee —, — tools.
5. The deer has a —, — fawn.
6. Our hens give us —, — eggs.
7. The men ate the —, — bread.

some	hungry	red	white	sweet
many	several	new	brown	stale
soft	wooden	old	metal	three
cold	spotted	two	small	large
blue	little	hot	fresh	lost

14. Using Words in Correct Order

In unit one, you learned that the words in a sentence must be in correct order. Read the three sentences below. Do you know which sentence has the words in the correct order?

Paul saw tiny, several yellow flowers.
Paul saw tiny, yellow several flowers.
Paul saw several tiny, yellow flowers.

The third sentence has the words in the correct order. In the third sentence, the number word **several** comes before the adjectives **tiny** and **yellow**.

What question does the word **several** answer? Read the sentences below. What question does the word in bold print in each sentence answer?

Mother found **two** ripe tomatoes.
Many old books are in the library.
Aunt Carol has **twelve** white hens.

Several, two, many, and **twelve** answer the question **how many**. When you use a word which tells **how many** with an adjective, always put the word which tells **how many** first.

▷ Oral Drill ▷

Use a word which tells **how many** to fill in the first blank in each sentence below. Use an adjective to fill in the second blank. Read each sentence correctly.

1. John has — — cows.
2. — — men helped the boys.
3. — — birds sang merrily.
4. Mother gave Amy — — towels.
5. Paul found — — chairs.
6. — — desks are in the garage.
7. — — flowers bloomed.

▷ For You to Do ▷

Copy each noun below. After each noun write a word to answer each question. Then write a sentence using the noun, and the words you used to answer the questions, together.

1. trees—how many? what size?
   trees—many, tall
   We saw <u>many</u> <u>tall</u> trees.
2. kittens—how many? what color?
3. trucks—how many? what size?
4. boys—how many? what kind?
5. boxes—how many? what shape?
6. lions—how many? what size?

15. Reviewing What We
Have Learned

> Oral Drill

A. Read each pair of sentences below. Then combine the two sentences in each pair to make one sentence which says the same thing.

1. The boys helped us. The boys were kind.

2. The horse neighed. The horse was hungry.

3. The man prayed. The man was thankful.

4. The clock stopped. The clock was old.

5. The wood burned. The wood was dry.

6. The dog whined. The dog was hurt.

7. The tiger roared. The tiger was angry.

8. The moon shone. The moon was bright.

B. Use adjectives and number words to complete each sentence below. Read each sentence correctly.

1. Samuel found —— —— saws.

2. —— —— girls sang songs.

3. Father has —— —— horses.

4. —— —— ducks were at the pond.

5. Mark's dog has —— —— puppies.

6. —— —— butterflies rested on the grass.

7. —— —— melons are on the vine.

8. —— —— boys mowed the lawn.

Written Practice

A. Write a sentence to go with each picture below. Use a number word and an adjective in each sentence.

1.

2.

3.

4.

5.

6.

7.

8.

B. Check your work for part A. Underline the adjective in each sentence. Draw a circle around the number word.

16. Meeting More Verbs

Every complete sentence has a verb. Can you find the verb in the sentence below?

I am thirsty.

The word **I** is a pronoun. The word **I** cannot be used as a verb. The word **thirsty** is an adjective. The word **thirsty** cannot be used as a verb. What word is left?

The word **am** is a verb. The word **am** does not show action the way some verbs do, but it is still a verb. There are other verbs which do not show action. The words **is** and **are** are two more verbs which do not show action.

 He **is** happy.
They **are** quiet.

Do you know how to use the verbs **am, is,** and **are** correctly? Use **am** when you are talking about yourself.

I **am** in second grade.
I **am** eight years old.

Use **is** when you are talking about only one person or thing.

The Bible **is** God's Word.
Sister Lois **is** patient.

Use **are** when you are talking about more than one person or thing, or with the pronoun **you.**

 The cows **are** in the barn.
You **are** my teacher.

Oral Drill

Use **am**, **is**, or **are** to complete each sentence.

1. God —— great.
2. I —— here.
3. You —— tired.
4. The trees —— old.
5. Jacob —— kind.

6. —— you ready?
7. —— I happy?
8. —— he a teacher?
9. I —— in school.
10. Mice —— rodents.

For You to Do

A. Use **is** or **are** to complete each sentence below. Write each sentence correctly.

1. God —— holy.
2. Grandfather —— old.
3. Wrens —— small.
4. Patty —— polite.
5. You —— helpful.

B. Draw a circle around the adjectives in part A.

C. Write three sentences about yourself. Use the verb **am** in each sentence.

17. *Was* **and** *Were*

You learned that some verbs do not show action. **Am, is,** and **are** are three verbs which do not show action. Now you will meet two more verbs which do not show action.

Read the two sentences below. Can you find the verb in each sentence?

> **Susan was sick.**
> **The boys were helpful.**

The words **was** and **were** are verbs. **Was** and **were** are two more verbs which do not show action.

Do you know how to use the verbs **was** and **were** correctly? Use **was** when you are talking about only one person or thing. Say:

> I **was** in first grade last year.
> That big cat **was** once a little kitten.

Use the verb **were** when you are talking about more than one person or thing, or when you are using the pronoun **you**. Never use **was** with the pronoun **you**. Say:

> You **were** my teacher last year.
> Father and Mother **were** in town.
> Several ducks **were** on the pond.

▷ Oral Drill ▷

Use **was** or **were** to complete each sentence.

1. You —— at home last night.

2. Mary —— in sixth grade.

3. The leaves —— pretty last fall.

4. Some of them —— yellow.

5. —— you ever at a zoo?

6. We —— there last summer.

7. A big lion —— in a cage.

8. My sister —— afraid of the lion.

9. Our cousins —— with us.

10. —— Paul in school last week?

> For You to Do >

A. Use **was** or **were** to complete each sentence below. Write each sentence correctly.

1. Miriam —— Aaron's sister.

2. Peter and Andrew —— brothers.

3. Mary and Elizabeth —— cousins.

4. Noah —— Shem's father.

5. Lois —— Timothy's grandmother.

6. Jonathan and David —— friends.

B. Write two telling sentences. Begin each sentence with the words **You were.**

C. Write two question sentences. Begin each question with the words **Were you.**

18. Present and Past

Read the sentences below.

I am in second grade.
You are my teacher.
The sun is hot.

Each of the above sentences is happening at the present time. You could add the word **now** to each sentence, and it would still make sense.

Look at the above sentences. Find the verbs **am, is**, and **are**. The verbs **am, is**, and **are** let us know that the sentences tell about the present time. The verbs **am, is**, and **are** are only used to tell about the present time.

Some sentences do not tell about the present time. Some sentences tell about the past.

Yesterday I was tired.
We were in first grade last year.

Each of the two sentences above tells about the past. The words **yesterday** and **last year** help us know that the sentences tell about the past. But we do not need these words to know that a sentence tells about the past.

Find the verbs in the two sentences above. The verbs are **was** and **were**. **Was** and **were** are only used to tell about the past. When we see **was** or **were**, we know that the sentence tells about the past.

Oral Drill

Find the verb in each sentence below. Then tell whether the sentence tells about the **present** or about the **past**.

1. He was hungry.
2. They were sick.
3. We are happy.
4. I am here.
5. You were busy.

6. She is kind.
7. They are quiet.
8. I was at home.
9. It is soft.
10. We were tired.

For You to Do

A. Use **am, is,** or **are** to make each sentence below tell about the present. Write each sentence correctly.

1. This soup —— delicious.
2. Penguins —— birds.
3. I —— a child.
4. The boys —— outside.

B. Use **was** or **were** to make each sentence below tell about the past. Write each sentence correctly.

1. The moon —— bright last night.
2. You —— at church.
3. The windows —— shut.
4. One door —— open.

19. More Work With *Present* and *Past*

The verbs **am**, **is**, and **are** help us tell about the present time. We should only use the verbs **am, is,** and **are** when we are talking about the present time.

Read the sentences below. Each sentence tells about the present time.

I **am** in school.
I **am** a child.

The sky **is** cloudy.
Philip **is** quiet.

You **are** ready to study.
The baby chicks **are** soft and fuzzy.

The verbs **was** and **were** help us tell about the past. We should only use the verbs **was** and **were** when we are telling about the past.

Read the sentences below. Each sentence tells about the past.

The watermelon **was** ripe.
Robert **was** absent yesterday.

Janet and Karen **were** in the kitchen.
Two horses **were** in the meadow.

⊃ Oral Drill ⊃

A. Use **am, is,** or **are** to make each sentence below tell about the present.

1. Jason —— friendly.
2. I —— not finished.
3. You —— thankful.
4. The pigs —— dirty.
5. The water —— hot.
6. You —— cheerful.
7. One cow —— black.
8. They —— late.
9. We —— children.
10. Ruth —— inside.

B. Use **was** or **were** to make each sentence above tell about the past.

⊃ For You to Do ⊃

Use **am, is, are, was,** or **were** to complete each sentence below. Write each sentence correctly.

1. Father —— home now.
2. He —— at the store earlier.
3. I —— ready to leave now.
4. I —— ready ten minutes ago.
5. You —— quiet last evening.
6. The boys —— in school now.
7. We —— at church yesterday.
8. You —— eight years old now.

20. Reviewing What We Have Learned

$\gt$ Oral Drill $\gt$

A. Find the verb in each sentence below. Then tell whether the sentence is telling about the **present** or about the **past**.

1. Brother Jacob is our minister.
2. The weather was cold.
3. The birds were hungry.
4. I am not in the fourth grade.
5. Susan and Kathy are sisters.
6. Some lizards were under the rock.
7. A toad was in our garden.
8. Some snakes are poisonous.
9. A black snake is helpful.
10. These blankets were in the attic.

B. Use **am, is, are, was,** and **were** to complete each sentence.

1. The boys —— helping Father now.
2. The girls —— helping Mother yesterday.
3. Last summer we —— in Canada.
4. Now we —— living in Ohio.
5. I —— studying English now.
6. Our teacher —— teaching us now.
7. Carl —— in sixth grade last year.

8. Where —— you last night

> Written Practice >

A. On your paper write the verb which correctly completes each sentence below.

1. Where (was, were) you this morning?
2. I (am, is) in school now.
3. Jacob (was, is) at home yesterday.
4. Last year they (was, were) at Uncle Ben's.
5. You (is, are) a good friend.
6. (Is, Am) Mary your sister?
7. Philip and James (is, are) her brothers.
8. Two deer (was, were) in our garden.
9. (Were, Was) they eating the corn?
10. One deer (was, were) eating strawberries.
11. A dog (is, was) barking now.
12. Last night the crickets (are, were) singing.
13. Two crickets (is, are) in our basement.
14. Our kitten (are, is) black and white.
15. The kitten's mother (was, were) white.

B. Use each of the verbs below in a sentence.

am   is   are   was   were

21. *Have* and *Has*

The words **have** and **has** are verbs. The verbs **have** and **has** are used in the sentences below.

Jacob **has** a Bible.
His Bible **has** a black cover.

I **have** two sisters.
My sisters **have** brown eyes.
Paul, you **have** blue eyes.

Do you know when to use **have** and **has**? Use **have** with the pronoun **I** and with the pronoun **you**. Also, use **have** when you are talking about more than one person or thing.

> I **have** a new book.
> **You have** a brother.
> The **boys have** a red wagon.

Use **has** when you are talking about only one person or thing, but **never** with the words **I** and **you**.

> **Carl has** a little pony.
> Our **house has** a chimney.
> **She has** a green dress.

> Oral Drill >

Practice using **have** and **has**.

1. Think about different things that you have. Take turns in class using sentences to tell what you have. Begin each sentence with the words **I have**.

2. Think about different things your school **has**. Take turns using sentences to tell what the school has. Try to use an adjective or number word in each sentence.

> Example: Our school **has** many large
> windows.

> For You to Do >

A. On your paper write whether you would use **have** or **has** to complete each sentence below.

1. You —— a dog.   5. A bird —— wings.
2. Mary —— a car.   6. I —— a pen.
3. He —— a cold.   7. They—— a tractor.
4. We —— friends.   8. Phil —— a horse.

B. Write six sentences using **have** or **has**. Use the words below to begin each sentence.

1. Mother . . .   4. You . . .
2. The girls . . .   5. A horse . . .
3. I . . .   6. The apple trees . . .

22. *Have, Has,* **and** *Had*

You learned that some verbs are used to tell about the present and some verbs are used to tell about the past. **Am, is,** and **are** are three verbs that are used to tell about the present. **Was** and **were** are two verbs that are used to tell about the past.

The verbs **have** and **has** are used to tell about the present. When we use the verbs **have** and **has,** we are talking about something that is **now.**

I **have** a gray coat.
The cow **has** a new calf.

The word **had** is a verb, also. When we use **had,** we are talking about the past. The verb **had** is used in each sentence below. Each sentence below tells about the past.

Last week, Martha **had** a cold.
The men **had** a meeting yesterday.
I **had** a birthday last month.
We **had** much snow last winter.

Remember to use **have** and **has** if you are talking about the present. Use the verb **had** when you are talking about the past.

> Oral Drill >

A. Use **have** or **has** to complete each sentence below.

1. I — a coat.
2. You — a cap.
3. He — shoes.
4. She — a pony.
5. It — a door.
6. We — a school.
7. They — apples.
8. The dog — a bone.

B. Use **had** to make each sentence above tell about the past.

> For You to Do >

A. Use **have, has,** or **had** to complete each sentence below. Write the correct verb on your paper.

1. Twenty years ago, Grandfather — a buggy.
2. Now he — an automobile.
3. Aunt Betty — white hair now.
4. She — black hair several years ago.
5. The cherry trees — blossoms now.
6. Last summer we — many cherries.

B. Write six sentences. Use each of the verbs below twice.

have   has   had

23. Thinking About Verbs

Let us think about some things we have learned about verbs. You have learned that some verbs show **action**.

The children **walk.**   A dog **barks.**
The people **pray.**   The girl **worked.**

You learned that the words **am, is, are, was,** and **were** are verbs. **Am, is,** and **are** tell about the present. **Was** and **were** tell about the past.

I **am** busy.   I **was** tired last night.
You **are** quiet.   They **were** patient yesterday.
She **is** my friend.

You learned that the words **have, has,** and **had** are verbs also. **Have** and **has** are used to tell about the present, and **had** is used to tell about the past.

You **have** some work to do now.
Keith **has** the measles now.
Pam **had** the measles last week.

In our English language, every complete sentence has a verb. When you write a sentence, check to be certain that you have used a verb. Check to be certain that you have used the verb **correctly.**

> For You to Do >

A. Find the verb in each sentence below. Write the verbs on your paper.

1. Some butterflies have yellow wings.

2. Moths and butterflies are insects.

3. Many insects eat leaves.

4. A locust has sharp jaws.

5. Locusts were a plague in Egypt.

6. They ate the leaves of the plants.

7. The locusts destroyed the crops of grain.

8. A spider is not an insect.

9. A spider has eight legs and no wings.

10. God made the many spiders and insects.

B. Write six sentences. Use two verbs from each group below.

Group 1		Group 2	
see	sings	am	was
run	works	is	were
came	played	are	

Group 3

have   has   had

24. More Practice With Verbs

Every complete sentence has a verb. Some sentences have more than one verb. Read the sentences below. Each of them has more than one verb.

> Kathy **washed** and **dried** the dishes.
> Tim **mowed** and **raked** the lawn.

Each sentence above has two verbs to tell what was done. In each sentence, the same person did both things. The first sentence tells us that Kathy washed the dishes **and** Kathy dried the dishes. The second sentence tells us that Tim mowed the lawn **and** Tim raked the lawn.

Read the two sentences below. Can you think of how we could write the same two thoughts using only one sentence?

> Mother **ironed** the clothes.
> Mother **folded** the clothes.

Both sentences tell us **Mother** did something. Both sentences tell us that Mother did something with **the clothes.** The first sentence uses the verb **ironed.** The second sentence uses the verb **folded.** We could combine the two sentences this way:

> Mother ironed **and** folded the clothes.

> Oral Drill >

Read each pair of sentences. Combine the two sentence thoughts to make one sentence, using the pattern given in the lesson.

1. Tom smiled. Tom laughed.
2. Jane slipped. Jane fell.
3. God sees us. God hears us.
4. We honor our parents. We obey our parents.
5. Uncle Mark knows God's promises. Uncle Mark believes God's promises.

> For You to Do >

A. Find the two verbs used in each sentence below. Write the verbs on your paper.

1. Kevin cleaned and swept the car.
2. The boys cut and stacked the wood.
3. Karen scrubbed and mopped the floor.
4. Father makes and repairs furniture.
5. The flowers wilted and died in the heat.

B. Combine the two sentence thoughts in each pair below to make one sentence. Write the new sentence on your paper.

1. The women sang. The women prayed.
2. Lee picked a pear. Lee ate a pear.
3. David loved God. David feared God.
4. Paul read the Bible. Paul studied the Bible.

25. Reviewing What We Have Learned

▷ Oral Drill ▷

A. Use **have** or **has** to complete each sentence below.

1. The boys —— new shoes.
2. Grandmother —— twenty-two grandchildren.
3. I —— three books about birds.
4. You —— an apple in your lunch.
5. Uncle Ben —— a dark blue car.
6. Our oak tree —— many acorns on it.
7. David and Carl —— a brown and white dog.
8. Lena —— three brothers and two sisters.

B. Combine the two sentence thoughts in each pair of sentences below to make one sentence.

1. Glen dropped the dish. Glen broke the dish.
2. The horses sniffed the oats. The horses ate the oats.
3. Clara washed the floor. Clara waxed the floor.
4. Luke raked the hay. Luke baled the hay.
5. James fed the cows. James milked the cows.
6. Mary opened the door. Mary shut the door.
7. Squirrels gather nuts. Squirrels bury nuts.

> **Written Practice** >

A. On your paper write the verbs found in the sentences below. After each verb, write whether the sentence is telling about the **present** or the **past**.

   1. The boys had twelve large, red apples.
   2. I am the oldest child in my family.
   3. That car has a flat tire.
   4. The chickens are in their pen.
   5. The cows were by the creek.
   6. Our house is white and gray.
   7. The girls have a surprise for Mother.
   8. A deer was in the field.

B. On your paper write a verb which you could correctly use to complete each sentence below.

   1. Lemons —— sour.   5. The men —— to God.
   2. Sugar —— sweet.   6. A dog ——.
   3. Eva —— a book.   7. I —— a plum.
   4. Children ——.   8. Tom —— a truck.

C. Write three sentences. Use two of the verbs below together in each sentence.

washed	obey	smiled	swept
waved	dried	cleaned	trust

Review One

> Oral Drill >

A. What are some words which you could use to tell:

1. what color? 3. what size?

2. what kind? 4. how many?

B. Use adjectives and number words to complete the sentences below.

1. Michael has a —— —— dog.
2. We have —— chickens.
3. —— books fell off the desk.
4. A mouse is ——.
5. The apples are ——.
6. God is ——.
7. —— —— rabbits are in the garden.
8. The horses are —— and ——.
9. We heard a —— siren.
10. My cousins live in a —— —— house.
11. The —— girl spoke in a —— voice.
12. The —— knife cut the —— bread.
13. Mother mended my —— —— coat.
14. The —— birds looked for food.
15. Brother Isaac is a —— man.

> **Written Practice** >

A. Copy the adjectives and number words which you find in the phrases below. Underline the number words.

1. wild lions
2. green leaves
3. round oranges
4. soft feathers
5. strong hands

6. two crisp cookies
7. one little puppy
8. tiny pink roses
9. five helpful boys
10. many tall trees

B. Use a word which tells how many to fill in the first blank in each sentence below. Use an adjective to fill in the second blank. Write the sentences correctly.

1. —— —— crows were in the field.
2. Mary picked —— —— flowers.
3. Jacob ate —— —— pancakes.
4. —— —— peaches are on the tree.
5. Father planted —— —— trees.

C. On your paper write the noun **kitten**. Then write three adjectives which you could use to tell about a kitten.

Can you think of more than three adjectives? Write any more that you can think of also.

Review Two

A. Use each of these verbs in a sentence:

is   am   are   was   were   have   has   had

B. Use one of the verbs above to make each sentence below tell about the present.

1. I —— here.   4. I —— a pear.
2. They —— a ball.   5. Lois —— a cold.
3. Eva —— at home.   6. You —— busy.

C. Use a verb from part A to make each sentence above tell about the past.

D. Use two verbs together to complete each sentence below. Can you think of more than one way to complete each sentence?

1. Lois —— and —— the dress.
2. David —— and —— the puppy.
3. The boys —— and —— the garden.
4. Terry —— and —— the dishes.
5. Tina —— and —— the eggs.
6. In the summer we —— and ——.
7. Mother —— and —— a cake.
8. The happy girls —— and ——.

> Written Practice >

A. On your paper, write the verb used in each sentence below. After each verb, write whether the sentence tells about the present or the past.

1. Last week I was in school.
2. Sarah and Anna have three brothers.
3. Their father had five sisters.
4. Their grandmother has a very old Bible.
5. The boys are in the attic.
6. I am not in the fourth grade.
7. Some rabbits were in the garden.
8. The minister's name is Henry Martin.

B. Rewrite each pair of sentences below as one sentence.

1. Father fixes cars. Father paints cars.
2. The sun rises. The sun sets.
3. Jane poured some milk. Jane drank some milk.
4. The women sang. The women prayed.

C. On your paper, write a verb which could be used to complete each sentence below.

1. The roses —— pink.
2. The bush —— thorns.
3. The thorns —— me.
4. The stars ——.
5. God —— the stars.

Extra Activity

Making A Poster

Use a large piece of heavy, colored paper. Across the top write your title. Choose one of these:

God Made Many Plants
God Made Many Animals

Find pictures of animals or plants to paste on your poster. Under each picture write a noun to name what is being shown. Write an adjective with each noun to describe what you see. For example, you might write:

red tulips   tall giraffe

A Poem to Enjoy

Gifts of Love

For my home and parents' care,
For food to eat and clothes to wear,
For loving friends and happy hours,
The song of birds and fragrant flowers;
Dear Father, watching from above,
I thank Thee for these gifts of love.

—Mayflower

Discussing the poem:

1. What are some things for which the poet is thankful?

2. Whom does the poet thank for these things?

3. Why do you think the poet calls these things, "gifts of love"?

Unit V

Using Our Language

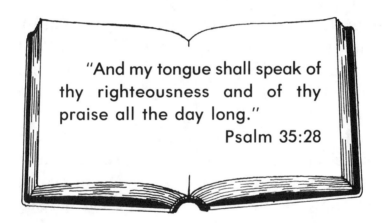

"And my tongue shall speak of thy righteousness and of thy praise all the day long."

Psalm 35:28

1. What Is a *Paragraph?*

Yesterday our family planted peas. Father marked the rows. Mother and I dropped the seeds into each row. Then Mark covered the seeds with the soil.

Look at the group of sentences above. The group of sentences above is called a **paragraph.** Do you know what a paragraph is?

A paragraph is a group of sentences which work together to tell about one subject. The sentences above tell about a family planting peas.

A paragraph must be written in a special way. Look at the paragraph at the top of this page. The first line begins a little farther from the edge of the page than the other lines do. We say that the first line is **indented.**

Find the paragraphs on this page. Look for the lines which are indented. Just as we use a capital letter to let us know where a new sentence begins, we indent a line to let us know where a new paragraph begins.

Look at the paragraphs on this page again. Except for the first line, the left side of each paragraph is kept straight. The right side is kept as straight as possible.

⟩ Class Activity ⟩

Find the last story you read in your reading book. Look at the paragraphs in the story. Do you see how the first line in each paragraph is indented? How many paragraphs are there? Is the left side kept straight? Is the right side made as straight as possible?

> **For You to Do** >

A. 1. Find the first story in your reading book.
   2. On your paper, write the first word of each paragraph.
   3. How many paragraphs are there?

B. The sentences below are not written as a paragraph. Write them carefully in the form of a paragraph. Remember to **indent** the first line. Keep the left side very straight. Make the right side as straight as possible.

1. A giraffe is a very tall animal.
2. It has a long neck and long legs.
3. It uses its long neck to reach the leaves on high trees.

2. What the Paragraph Is About

A paragraph is a group of sentences which work together to tell about one **subject**. Read the paragraph below. Can you decide what the **subject** of the paragraph is?

> **Last Saturday our family had a picnic indoors. Our kitchen table had broken, so Mother spread an old quilt on the floor. We all sat on the quilt and ate our supper.**

Look at the first sentence of the paragraph above. The first sentence tells us that a family had a picnic indoors. The second and third sentences tell more about the picnic. They help explain why and how the family had a picnic indoors.

All the sentences in the paragraph work together to tell about one subject. All of the sentences work together to tell about the family's picnic.

Which of the titles below would best tell the subject of the paragraph?

**An Indoor Picnic
My Family
Our Table**

An Indoor Picnic would be a good title because it tells what the main subject of the paragraph is.

> **For You to Do** >

A. Read each paragraph below. Then choose which title best fits the paragraph. Write the correct title on your paper.

1. Last week one of our cows had twin calves. Jacob and I named the small, spotted one Tiny. We named the black one Midnight.
   a. Blackie
   b. Two New Calves
   c. My Brother

2. Snowflake is our pet rabbit. She is all white except for her pink eyes. Whenever we give her cabbage leaves, Snowflake sits up and wiggles her nose.
   a. In the Garden
   b. A New Kitten
   c. Snowflake

B. Write the sentences below as a paragraph.

1. Yesterday our cousins came to visit us.

2. We took turns sledding down the big hill behind the barn.

3. Then we went indoors, and Mother gave us some hot milk and fresh cookies.

3. Finding the Subject of the Paragraph

> Hummingbirds are the smallest birds that God made. Most of them are only three inches long. One kind of hummingbird is only as big as a bumblebee.

Read the paragraph above carefully. What do you think the subject of the paragraph is? Which title below would best fit the paragraph?

> **Bumblebees**
> **Robins and Sparrows**
> **The Smallest Birds**

The paragraph mentions a bumblebee, but it is not about bumblebees. The paragraph is about birds, but it is not about robins and sparrows.

The paragraph is about hummingbirds, the smallest birds that God made. The title **The Smallest Birds** tells us what the subject of the paragraph is.

> Class Activity >

Read the following paragraphs carefully. Then decide what the subject of each paragraph is.

A. The ostrich is the largest bird God made. Some ostriches grow to be eight feet tall. They might weigh as much as three hundred pounds.

B. Owls are nighttime birds. They sleep during the day and hunt food during the night. Their sharp eyes help them find mice and insects even when it is dark.

> **For You to Do** >

A. Decide which title below best fits paragraph A in Class Activity. Write the correct title on your paper.

1. Little Birds
2. The Ostrich
3. Elephants

B. Decide which of the titles below best fits paragraph B. Write the title correctly on your paper.

1. Birds of the Night
2. Mice
3. In the Day

C. Write the sentences below in the form of a paragraph. Remember to indent the first line.

1. Penguins are sometimes called "Birds of the Sea."

2. They can swim very well, but they cannot fly at all.

3. In the water they catch fish and other animals to eat.

4. More Practice Finding the Subject

Read carefully the following paragraph. Try to decide what the subject of the paragraph is.

> One kind of lizard, a chameleon, can change color. It will look green when it is on the green grass. When it moves to a brown log, it will turn brown.

What is the first sentence of the paragraph about? It is about a kind of lizard called a chameleon (kə•mē′lē•ən). Does the second sentence tell about the chameleon also? Does the third sentence?

All three sentences work together to tell about the chameleon. The chameleon is the subject of the paragraph.

> **Class Activity**

Read the following paragraphs carefully. Then decide what the subject of each paragraph is.

A. Alligators and crocodiles do not really look alike. An alligator has a short, square snout. The snout of a crocodile is long and pointed.

B. Toads are good helpers to have in the garden. They eat the slugs that can hurt the cabbage plants. They also eat many harmful insects.

C. The leatherback is a large sea turtle. Instead of a hard shell, it has a tough, leathery skin. Some leatherbacks grow to be over eight feet long.

> For You to Do >

A. Copy the titles below correctly. After each title write **A, B,** or **C** to tell which paragraph from above the title best fits.

1. A Large Sea Turtle
2. Alligators and Crocodiles
3. How Toads Help Us

B. Write the sentences below as a paragraph. Then copy the title which best tells the subject of the paragraph.

1. Jason has a pet turtle.
2. He keeps it in a large box.
3. Every day he feeds it earthworms, insects, or scraps of meat.

   a. A Large Box
   b. Jason's Pet Turtle
   c. Earthworms

5. Reviewing What We Have Learned

▷ Class Activity ▷

A. Discuss what makes a group of sentences a paragraph.

B. Read carefully the following paragraphs. Then decide what the subject of each paragraph is.

1. Last spring, Mary and I visited Uncle Roy's sheep farm. We watched him cut the wool off the sheep. We helped him feed some of the baby lambs.

2. Uncle Roy has a dog named Shep. Shep helps Uncle Roy take care of the sheep. If a sheep wanders too far, Shep runs after it and brings it back.

3. Uncle Roy gave us two lambs. They were both dark brown. We named them Coffee and Chocolate.

4. Aunt Carol keeps some of the sheep wool. First she washes it carefully. Then she combs it and spins it into yarn. She uses the yarn to make warm socks and mittens.

> Written Practice >

A. Find the second story in your reading book. Then answer the questions below.

1. What is the first word of each paragraph?

2. How many paragraphs are there?

3. How many sentences are in the first paragraph?

B. Copy the titles given below. After each title write **1, 2, 3,** or **4** to tell which paragraph on the previous page the title best fits.

A Dog Named Shep   Coffee and Chocolate

Using the Wool   A Visit to a Sheep Farm

C. Write the sentences below in the form of a paragraph. Then choose the title which best tells the subject of the paragraph. Copy the title correctly.

1. Aunt Carol is our sunshine aunt.

2. She is always very happy.

3. No matter what happens, she sings songs and praises God.

   a. Going to Sunday School

   b. All the Time

   c. Our Sunshine Aunt

6. Finding the Paragraph's Subject

The sentences in a paragraph should all work together to tell about one subject. When you want to know what the subject of a paragraph is, you must decide what one thing all the sentences tell about.

Read the following paragraph carefully.

> **The blue whale is the largest animal that God made. It can grow to be over one hundred feet long. Some blue whales weigh as much as thirty elephants. Even a baby blue whale is larger than a full-grown elephant.**

Now go back and read the first sentence. What does the first sentence tell us? It tells us that the blue whale is the largest animal.

Now read the second sentence. What does it tell us? It tells us about the blue whale also. It helps explain the first sentence by telling us how long a blue whale might be.

Read the third and fourth sentences. They tell us how much a blue whale can weigh and how big a baby blue whale is.

All four sentences work together to tell about the size of a blue whale. We could say that the subject of the paragraph is The Largest Animal or The Size of the Blue Whale.

> Class Activity >

Find the subject of the paragraph below. First read the paragraph carefully. Then go back and read each sentence. Decide what one subject all the sentences tell about.

An ostrich egg is much larger than a chicken egg. Most ostrich eggs weigh about four pounds. Some ostrich eggs are as big as a man's head.

> For You to Do >

A. Read the paragraph below carefully. Then go back and read each sentence. Decide what the one subject is which all the sentences tell about. Write the subject of the paragraph on your paper.

God made different kinds of flowers to bloom at different times. Tulips, lilacs, and daffodils bloom in the springtime. Asters and marigolds bloom in the summer and fall. The bright red poinsettias (poin•set′ē•əz) bloom in the winter time.

B. In the paragraph above, find the **six nouns** which name different kinds of flowers. Write these nouns on your paper.

7. More Work Finding the Subject

Some paragraphs tell about similar things. Read the two paragraphs below. They both have similar subjects, but the subjects are not exactly the same. Can you tell how they are different?

Elephants are very large. They are the largest animal which lives on land. Some elephants weigh as much as six tons, or 12,000 pounds!

Elephants are very strong animals. With their heads they can push down tall trees that are two feet thick. With their trunks, they can carry large logs.

Both paragraphs are about elephants. The first paragraph tells us about **the size of an elephant**. The second paragraph tells us that **elephants are very strong**.

When you read a paragraph, try to decide exactly what it is telling about. If two paragraphs tell about similar things, try to decide how the subject of each paragraph is different.

> Class Activity >

Read the two paragraphs below. Decide what the subject of each paragraph is. Tell how the subject of each paragraph is different.

A. Polar bears live where it is very cold. Their thick coat protects them from the cold wind and snow. Stiff fur on the bottoms of their feet keeps them from slipping on the ice.

B. Polar bears are good swimmers. They can swim far out in the ocean. When they get tired, they climb onto a floating block of ice.

> For You to Do >

A. On your paper, write what you think would be a good title for the paragraph below.

> With our feet and legs, we can move in different ways. Sometimes we walk, skip, or run. At other times we jump or hop.

B. In the paragraph above, find the five verbs which tell different ways that we move. Write the five verbs on your paper.

8. Writing Sentences in Order

When we write a sentence, we must be careful to put the words in correct order. When we write a paragraph, we must be careful to put the sentences in correct order.

If you wanted to eat an apple, which of these things would you do first? second? third?

wash the apple
cut the apple
eat the apple

First you would wash the apple, and then cut it. Finally you would eat it.

Read the paragraph below. It tells about eating apples. Notice what happens in each sentence. Do you think the sentences are in correct order?

> **Mother washed several apples. She cut them into pieces. We each ate four pieces.**

The first sentence tells about washing the apples. The second sentence tells about cutting the apples. The third sentence tells about eating the apples. The three sentences are written in the correct order.

▷ Class Activity ▷

For each group of sentences below, decide which sentence tells about what happened first. Then decide which sentence tells about what happened next and which tells about what happened last. Read the sentences in the correct order.

A. 1. We pulled weeds during the summer.

2. In the fall we picked the ripe pumpkins.

3. In the spring we planted pumpkin seeds.

B. 1. She used the mashed pumpkin to make pies.

2. Mother cleaned the pumpkins.

3. She cooked and mashed them.

▷ For You to Do ▷

A. Decide in which order the things mentioned in the sentences below happened. Put the sentences in correct order. Write them in paragraph form.

1. Mother used them to make muffins.

2. Father and I picked the blueberries.

3. Mother and Hope cleaned them.

B. Write a title which would tell the subject of the paragraph you wrote for part A.

9. More Practice With Sentence Order

Think about some things that you do in school. Do you do these three things?

have devotions
do your reading lesson
eat lunch

In what order do you do the three things mentioned above? Which do you do first? second? third?

When you have devotions, what do you do? Do you sing, pray, and read the Bible? In what order do you do these things?

Here is a paragraph which tells how one class has devotions. Can you tell in what order the class does each thing?

> **Every morning we have devotions. First we sing a song. Then Sister Anna reads to us from the Bible. After that she leads us in prayer.**

Take time to observe the order in which things happen. Think about what happens first, second, and third. When you write about things that happened, be careful to write your sentences in the order in which each thing happened.

> Class Activity >

Think about some things that you have to do when you do the dishes. Tell each thing in the order in which it is done. See how many steps your class can think of. Here are some ideas to help you:

clear the table   put hot water in the sink
wash the dishes   put the dishes away

> For You to Do >

A. For each group of sentences below, write the letters of the sentences in the order in which the things told about happened.

1. a. We helped put the dough onto the pans.
   b. After the cookies were baked, we each ate one.
   c. Mother mixed some cookie dough.

2. a. Quickly Mark tagged Howard and Jesse.
   b. They chose Mark to be "It."
   c. The boys decided to play tag.

B. Write in paragraph form the sentences in **group 2** above. Remember to write the sentences in correct order.

C. Write a title which would tell the subject of the paragraph that you wrote for **part B**.

10. Reviewing What We Have Learned

> Class Activity

A. Read each group of sentences below. Then decide in what order each thing happened. Read the sentences again in correct order.

1. a. Father gave him some nails.
   b. Samuel asked Father for some nails.
   c. Samuel used them to fix the wagon.

2. a. They began to fall off the trees.
   b. Soon the lawn was covered with leaves.
   c. The leaves began to turn orange and yellow.

3. a. We raked the leaves into large piles.
   b. When we were done, Father carried the bags to the garden.
   c. Then we put the leaves into bags.

4. a. He found a squirrel caught in the rain spout.
   b. Father went outside.
   c. Last night we heard a strange noise.

B. Think of a title to go with each group of sentences above.

> **Written Practice** >

A. Copy these titles: A Visit to Uncle Ben's
                      Uncle Ben's Ponies
                      Where Uncle Ben Works

Decide which paragraph below goes with each title. Write the number of each paragraph after the correct title.

1. Uncle Ben works in the woods. He cuts down large trees. He sells the trees to a lumber company.

2. Uncle Ben has two large ponies. They help him do his work. He uses them to pull logs out of the woods.

3. Last week we visited Uncle Ben's. Father helped Uncle Ben with his work. Mother helped Aunt Susan. Lee and I helped our cousins rake the leaves.

B. Read the sentences below. Decide in what order the things told about happened. Write the sentences in correct order in paragraph form.

1. He took it to Mother.

2. Father found a lost puppy.

3. She gave it some warm milk.

C. Write a title to go with the paragraph you wrote in part B.

11. Sentences That Do Not Belong

The sentences in a paragraph should work together to tell about one subject. If a sentence does not tell about a paragraph's subject, it does not belong in the paragraph.

Read the paragraph below. Can you find the sentence which does not belong?

A Visit to the Zoo

Last summer we went to the zoo. We saw tigers, lions, and bears. Our cousins live in Canada. We saw many other animals also.

Three of the sentences tell about a visit to the zoo. One of the sentences does not tell about the zoo. The sentence, **Our cousins live in Canada**, does not tell about the visit to the zoo. The sentence about **our cousins** does not belong in the paragraph.

When you write a paragraph, check to be certain that all the sentences tell about one subject. Do not include any sentences which do not tell about the subject of the paragraph.

> Class Activity >

A. Read each paragraph below. In each paragraph, find the sentence which does not belong. Tell why it does not belong.

1. Hares are larger than rabbits. We plant a garden every year. They have larger feet and ears. Some hares may be more than two feet long.

2. The real name for a jack rabbit is a jack hare. They have very strong hind legs. Last month Grandfather visited us. Some jack hares can leap as far as twenty feet.

B. For each sentence below, give another sentence which would tell about the same thing.

1. On Sunday we go to church.

2. I am in the second grade.

3. God made many kinds of flowers.

> For You to Do >

Read the sentences below. Decide which one does not belong. Then write the sentences below in correct order in paragraph form. Leave out the sentence which does not belong.

1. Jason and I dried them.

2. Sarah washed the dishes.

3. Brother Lee is our music teacher.

4. Then Lois put them away.

12. Thinking About Things We See

Look at the picture at the top of this page. Study the picture carefully. Can you find the answers to these questions?

> **Is it cold? How do you know?**
> **How many children are there?**
> **What are the children doing?**

Read the two paragraphs below. Both of them tell about the picture. Which paragraph do you think tells us the most about the picture?

> **One day some children were outside. They were working.**

> **One warm day, a boy and two girls were working in the berry patch. They were busy picking the ripe, red strawberries.**

The first paragraph does not tell us exactly how many children there were. It does not tell us exactly where the children were or what they were doing.

The second paragraph uses exact words to tell about the children. It tells us that there were two girls and a boy. It tells us exactly where they were and what they were doing. The word **warm** is used to describe the day. The words **ripe** and **red** are used to describe the strawberries.

When you are looking at something, try to think of words which say exactly what you see. When you want to tell someone about something you saw, take time to think of exact words which will tell exactly what you saw.

⟩ Class Activity ⟩

In each set of words below, one word is more exact. Tell which word is more exact, and then use it in a sentence.

1. dogs—collies
2. apples—fruit
3. building—barn
4. moved—jumped
5. state—Ohio
6. hammer—tool

⟩ For You to Do ⟩

The paragraph below does not use very exact words. Use the words from the list below to take the place of the words in bold print. Rewrite the paragraph correctly.

One **time** we saw **some animals**. They were by the **water**. They **went** into the water and **went** away.

creek   beavers   dived   night   swam   three

13. Thinking About What We Hear

How well do you use your ears? How many sounds can you hear right now? Can you hear any of these things?

somebody talking　paper rustling
footsteps　a pencil being used

The sounds we hear help us know what is happening. When you hear the windows rattling at night, you might know that a strong wind is blowing. A popping sound in the kitchen might mean that someone is making popcorn.

When we tell about the sounds we hear, we should use exact words and phrases. Was the sound we heard **loud**, or **soft**? Did we hear a **scratching** noise, or a **banging** noise?

Sometimes we compare sounds that we hear to something else that we heard before. Read the paragraph below. The first sentence uses the words **strange** and **tapping** to describe the noise. The second sentence compares the noise to something that was heard before.

Last night I heard a strange tapping noise. It sounded like someone rapping on my window. When I looked, I saw what it was. It was a bird pecking at the insects on the window.

> Class Activity >

A. Tell what you might hear that would let you know:

1. that someone is at the door.
2. that someone is happy.
3. that it is raining.

B. What would you think might be happening if you were to hear:

1. a crash in the kitchen?
2. a scratching noise in the cupboard?
3. a car door being shut?

> For You to Do >

A. Copy the paragraph below. Use the words in bold print to help you decide what made the noise. Choose the best phrase from the list to complete the last sentence.

Last night Father heard a **soft, rustling** noise. He said that it sounded **like someone scratching at a piece of paper.** He went out to the kitchen. There he found ——.

a dog barking
a mouse in the cracker box
water dripping in the sink

B. List three things you hear when you are:

1. in church   2. outdoors

14. Thinking About Things
We Feel

Rub your hands over this page. How does it feel? Which of the words below would you use to describe how it feels?

bumpy   rough   smooth   scratchy   sticky

Most paper feels smooth, unless it is sandpaper. Sandpaper feels rough and scratchy. Tar paper feels sticky. Paper on which Braille (brāl) is written feels bumpy.

People who are blind read Braille. Braille is written by making tiny bumps in the paper. Blind people use their fingers to feel the bumps.

If you have eyes which work well, you do not need to use your fingers to feel what you read. But you must use your fingers to feel many other things.

How do you know if water is hot or cold? How do you know if a towel is wet or dry? Knowing whether something is wet, dry, hot, or cold is an example of something you learn by feeling.

Sometimes when we write, we describe how things feel. Read the sentences below. As you read each sentence, try to think how each thing described actually felt.

The summer sun felt **hot** on my face.
The **sharp** stones hurt our feet.
The **warm** taffy was still **sticky**.

▷ Class Activity ▷

A. Tell how each of these things might feel:

1. a feather
2. a thistle
3. a pinched finger
4. a blanket on a cold night
5. a blanket on a hot night

B. Use each word below in a sentence to describe how something feels.

> Example: **sharp**—The broken glass was **sharp**.
>
> round   hard   soft   itchy   slippery

▷ For You to Do ▷

Copy the paragraph below. Underline the four words which tell how something felt. Then choose a word from the list below the paragraph to complete the last sentence. Use the word which names what was being described.

> Jason put his hand into the box. Inside he felt something soft and fuzzy. When he squeezed it, it felt round and juicy. When he pulled his hand out, he was holding a ——.
>
> **stone   ball   pillow   peach   kitten**

15. Reviewing What We Have Learned

> Class Activity >

A. Look at the picture below. Use your eyes to find the answers to these questions:

1. What do you see happening?
2. How many different things can you find?
3. Is it cold? How do we know?
4. Is the dog friendly? How do we know?
5. Is there a fire burning in the house?

B. Describe some sounds that you might hear if you were one of the children in the picture.

C. Describe how some things might feel if you were one of the children in the picture.

▷ Written Practice ▷

A. Read each sentence below. On your paper write whether the sentence helps you **see**, **hear**, or **feel** what is being described. Take time to think about each sentence. Some of the sentences have more than one answer.

1. The rooster's loud crowing woke us.
2. The stones were hot and sharp under our bare feet.
3. The tall mountains were covered with snow.
4. The pink flowers were soft and smooth.
5. The smiling girl sang cheerfully.
6. We were quiet while Father prayed.
7. The cold wind rattled the windows.
8. The tiny, yellow chicks were soft and fluffy.

B. Write a sentence to describe:

1. something you **saw** on your way to school.
2. something you **heard** on your way to school
3. something you **felt** on your way to school.

16. Writing About What We See

How closely do you look at God's world? What do you see when you look at the grass in the early morning? Do you see each blade of grass and the many tiny insects? Do you see the finely spun spider webs and the little drops of dew?

God has made many marvelous things. If we use our eyes wisely, we will see more and more of God's wonderful works. Then, when we write, we will be able to tell others about some of the wonderful things we have seen which God has made.

We can use our eyes also to help us see what is happening. Look at your classroom. What is happening? Are the children studying? Is anyone at the blackboard? Is the sun shining through the windows?

To write a paragraph about what you see, first look closely. Make a list of the things you see and of what is happening. Write sentences which tell what you see. Choose words which will help say exactly what you see.

> Class Activity >

Write a paragraph together as a class. First walk quietly to the window. Look outside. Think about what you see.

Then go back to your seats. Take turns telling about what you saw. The teacher will make a list on the board. Use the list to help you write the paragraph.

> For You to Do >

Make a list of several things you see happening now in your classroom. Write a paragraph about your classroom, using your list to help you.

17. Writing About What We Hear

If we use our ears carefully, we can hear many different sounds. Outside we might hear birds singing or bees buzzing. Inside we might hear soup boiling or a clock ticking.

When we write about things we have heard, we should use words which will describe how each noise sounded. Some adjectives describe noise. **Loud** and **soft** are two adjectives we can use to tell how something sounded.

Some verbs help us explain how something sounds.

We **crunched** the carrots.
The water **dripped**.
The boys **panted**.
The gate **clicked**.

Crunched, dripped, panted, and **clicked** are verbs which make us think of certain sounds.

Read the paragraph below. As you read it, think of how each noise actually sounded.

> I lay in bed listening carefully. I could hear my sister breathing softly. In the bathroom, I could hear water dripping, drip-drip-drip. Outside I could hear a bird quietly calling, "Whip-poor-will, Whip-poor-will."

> Class Activity >

A. Some words are only used to tell about sounds. Read the words below. Tell what things might make the sounds described.

1. Clippety-clop!   4. Cluck, cluck!
2. Buzz, buzz!   5. Hiss!
3. Whoo-whoo!   6. Squish-squish!

B. Think about some sounds you might hear if you went to the city. Tell about the sounds in sentences. Try to use words which will tell exactly how each thing sounded.

> For You to Do >

Make a list of sounds you might hear if you were on a farm during the summer. Use your list to help you write a paragraph about **Farm Sounds.**

18. Writing About What We Feel

Did you ever hold a kitten in your arms? How did it feel? Was it soft and furry? Could you feel its heart beating? Maybe it scratched you a little with its claws.

Here is a paragraph which describes how a kitten felt to one person:

> I held the little kitten in my arms. I stroked its **soft fur**. The kitten started to **squirm around**. Its **sharp claws** accidentally **scratched** me.

The words in bold print help describe how the kitten felt. Do you think that these words would describe how all animals feel? Would they describe a bird, or a turtle?

When we describe a bird, we would probably say that it feels **feathery**. We might say that it **pecked** one of our fingers.

A turtle would feel **hard,** like a rock. Its feet and head would feel a little **rough.**

When you write about how something felt, you should use words which will help explain exactly how it felt. Choose words which will help the reader **feel** what you are describing.

Class Activity

Use a sentence to describe how each of these things would feel:

1. an ice cube   3. a puppy   5. molasses
2. mud puddles   4. mittens   6. grass

For You to Do

Look at the two pictures below. Think about what the boys in each picture might be feeling. Remember that they can feel with their feet and faces, too!

Write a paragraph about one of the pictures. Tell what you think you would be feeling if you were one of the boys.

19. Seeing, Hearing, and Feeling

Usually when we are using our eyes, we are using our ears also. Many times we are seeing, hearing, and feeling things all at the same time.

Sometimes when we write, we describe how something looked, sounded, and felt. Then we must choose words which will help the reader to **see, hear,** and **feel** what we are describing.

Read the paragraph below. It tells what one girl saw, heard, and felt when she was taking a trip.

> **Father turned onto the narrow, dirt road. I could hear the car splashing through the mud puddles. Slowly we bounced along the bumpy road, up and down, up and down.**

Here is another paragraph which describes something someone saw, heard, and felt.

> **When I go home, our collie always runs to meet me. He barks until I scratch his soft, furry ears. Then he wags his big brown tail back and forth.**

▷ Class Activity ▷

Think about the last time that you were on the playground.

1. What are some things you saw?
2. What are some things you heard?
3. What are some things you felt.

Write a paragraph together as a class to describe some things you heard, saw, and felt on the playground.

▷ For You to Do ▷

Write a paragraph about something you saw, heard, and felt. Below are some ideas to help you. You may write about one of them or about something else.

1. popcorn—little and white; popping; light and spongy
2. a fire—orange and yellow; crackling; hot
3. a chicken—its color; clucking; warm and soft; a sharp beak
4. a summer day—What did you see?
   What did you hear?
   What did you feel?

20. Reviewing What We Have Learned

> Class Activity >

A. Each of the verbs below can be used to tell about the sound that something made. What do you think might have made each sound?

1. roared
2. squeaked
3. banged

4. peeped
5. laughed
6. crashed

7. chirped
8. plopped
9. purred

B. Look at the picture below. Use sentences to tell about things you think the children in the picture might be seeing, hearing, and feeling.

> **Written Practice** >

A. Write these five nouns on your paper:

    water   toast   pigeon   frog   pancakes

    After each noun, write a word from column A to describe how the thing might look. Write a word from column B to describe how the thing might sound. Write a word from column C to tell how it might feel.

A	B	C
brown	sizzled	crisp
green	dripping	feathery
flat	croaked	smooth
clear	crunchy	spongy
gray	cooed	wet

B. Write a paragraph about something you have seen, heard, and felt. Maybe you will want to write about one of these subjects:

1. **My Pet**—What kind of pet is it? What does it look like? What sound does it make? How does it feel?

2. **Walking in the Rain**—What do you see? Can you hear the rain splashing? Do you hear your rubbers going squish-squish? Do you feel cold and damp?

21. Rhyming Words

When two words end with the same sound, we say that they rhyme. We use rhyming words when we write poems and songs. Read the poem below. The words are also the words to a well-known song.

> Jesus loves me, this I **know**,
> For the Bible tells me **so**.
> Little ones to him **belong**;
> They are weak but He is **strong**.

As you read the poem, could you hear the words which rhyme? The last words in the first and second line rhyme with each other. The last words in the third and fourth line rhyme with each other.

Some rhyming words end with different letters. **Know** and **so** end with different letters. Some rhyming words end with the same letters. **Belong** and **strong** end with the same letters.

To know if two words rhyme, do not **look** at them. Say the words. Listen to the end sounds. If they end with the same sound, then they are rhyming words.

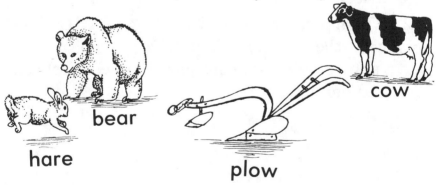

bear

hare

plow

cow

> For You to Do >

A. Copy each word below. Next to each word write a rhyming word found in the list below. Say the two words carefully to be certain that they end with the same sound.

1. wood   4. plan 7. chair
2. rude   5. two   8. lake
3. bat   6. so   9. tree

me   do   sat   food   stare
woe   could can   ache

B. Read the verses below. On your paper, write in pairs the words at the ends of the lines which rhyme.

Jesus loves me, He who died,
Heaven's gates to open wide;
He will wash away my sin,
Let His little child come in.

Jesus loves me, loves me still,
Though I'm very weak and ill;
From His shining throne on high,
Comes to watch me where I lie.

22. Using Rhyming Words

Using rhyming words helps make poetry sound pleasing. Read the verse below. Notice how the words in bold print have been changed so that they do not rhyme.

> Jesus loves me, this I know,
> For the Bible tells me **this**.
> Little ones to Him belong;
> They are weak but He is **mighty**.

The words mean the same, but they do not sound as pleasing. How much better the verse sounds to our ears when the words rhyme! When we write rhymes, we should take time to find good pairs of rhyming words. Then others will enjoy reading the words which we have written.

To choose a rhyming word, say the last sound of the word you want to rhyme. Think of other words which end with the same sound. If you are writing a rhyme, be certain that your rhyming word makes sense.

God made the sun to shine up high:
A yellow light in a bright, blue ? .

What word would rhyme with **high**? The word **high** ends with the **long i** sound. Here are some other words which end with the **long i** sound:

pie   sigh   tie   sky   firefly

Choose one of the rhyming words to help make a good rhyme. Remember to choose one which will make sense.

God made the sun to shine up **high**:
A yellow light in a bright, blue **sky**.

> For You to Do >

A. Copy each of the words below. Next to each write a word which rhymes. Say the words together to be certain that they end with the same sound.

1. light   4. blue   7. star
2. sea   5. seven   8. cost
3. bed   6. go   9. play

B. Read the verses below. Choose a word which rhymes with the word in bold print to complete each verse. Remember to use a word which makes sense. Write the verses on your paper.

1. Dear God, we thank You for the **breeze**
   Which softly whispers in the ——.

   sneeze   trees   flowers

2. Fresh snow is **bright**
   and very ——.

   soft   might   white

23. Finishing A Rhyme

Here is a poem which still needs to be finished. Can you think of a rhyming word to finish the last line?

God hears our prayers.
We know He ——.

In the poem above, the first line ends with the word **prayers**. Can you think of some words that rhyme with **prayers**?

stairs   pairs   cares   hares

Stairs, pairs, and **hares** rhyme, but they would not make sense in the poem. The word **cares** would be a good word to use. It rhymes with **prayers** and makes the poem make sense.

God hears our prayers.
We know He cares.

> Class Activity >

Use a rhyming word to finish each of the following poems.

1. God gave the sun to light the day,
   And stars at night to show the ——.

2. What do all God's creatures do,
   That are penned up in a ——.

3. Jesus is our Shepherd dear;
   We know that He is always ——.

4. God wants children to obey,
   When we work and when we ——.

5. I like to listen to the rain,
   Bouncing on the window ——.

> **For You to Do** >

Use a rhyming word to complete each poem below. Remember to use a word that makes sense. Write each poem correctly.

1. God made the little honey bee,
   Which makes such sweets for you and ——.

2. I love my father and my mother.
   I love my sister and my ——.

3. I saw some sparrows in the tree.
   I counted them, and there were ——.

24. Writing A Poem

Did you ever write a poem? Sometimes we write a poem when we make a card for somebody. Here is a poem which might have been written in a get-well card:

> We think about you every day,
> And remember you each time we pray.

Poems can be written about many things. Sometimes a poem is written about God, or about something God made.

> I am so glad that God above
> Is a God of power and love.

> God made the stars which shine so bright,
> Like little candles in the night.

Sometimes we write poems about things we saw or heard, or about something that happened.

> I heard a little chickadee
> Singing in the hemlock tree.

> Baby Jacob is my brother;
> I like to watch him for my mother.

When you want to write a poem, think of a subject to write about. Think of some rhyming words to use in your poem. Remember to use words which will make the poem make sense.

> Class Activity

Think of a second line to finish this rhyme:

God made the mountains and deep, wide seas,

_____ .

Can you think of more than one way to finish the rhyme?

> **For You to Do** >

A. Choose a pair of rhyming words from the list to complete each poem below. Write the poems on your paper. (You will not need to use all the rhyming words.)

1. I like to watch the kittens ——;
   They are so cuddly, soft, and ——.

2. My father said I ——
   To give my chickens ——.

need—feed   found—ground
eat—sweet   play—gray

B. Think of a second line to finish this rhyme. Write the rhyme correctly.

Jesus watches me each day,

_____.

25. Reviewing What We Have Learned

> **Class Activity**

A. Say each word below carefully. Then take turns saying words which rhyme with the words below.

1. sight   4. lake   7. hop   10. late
2. sea   5. seed   8. red   11. hay
3. old   6. care   9. joy   12. sew

B. Write a poem together as a class. Maybe your class will want to write about one of these subjects:

The Things God Made
What I Heard
Something I Saw

> **Written Practice**

A. On your paper, write the words from each group which rhyme.

1. cow   3. bear   5. cost
   how   hear   most
   show   dear   lost

2. rough   4. new   6. gone
   cough   blue   thrown
   off   sew   stone

B. Look at the picture below. Write five nouns to name things which you see in the picture. Next to each noun write a rhyming word.

C. Write a poem of your own. Maybe you will want to write about one of these subjects:

Summer Days

Winter Fun

God's Gifts to Me

If there is time, you might want to make a card. Fold a clean piece of paper in half. Put a picture on the outside. Write your rhyme neatly on the inside. Give the card to a friend, a relative, or someone who is sick.

Review One

A. Answer these questions:

1. What is a paragraph?

2. How do we know when a new paragraph begins?

B. Read each paragraph below. Tell what the subject of each paragraph is.

1. Carl has a pet frog. He named it Jumper. He feeds Jumper flies and other insects. Sometimes he takes Jumper to the garden. Then Jumper can catch his own food.

2. Last spring we had a flood. It rained and rained. The water came into our house. We could not drive our car because the water was too deep.

3. Sally is my little sister. She does not go to school yet because she is only three years old. Most of the time she spends playing house with her doll.

4. We have some little helpers in our garden. They are called ladybugs. They eat aphids, fleas, and other tiny insects.

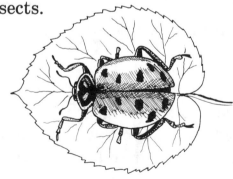

> **Written Practice** >

A. From the list, choose the best title to go with the paragraph. Write the title correctly on your paper.

> Yesterday I helped Mother make tomato juice. First we washed and cooked the tomatoes. Then I pushed the tomatoes through a strainer. Mother poured the fresh tomato juice into clean jars.

    a. Working in the Garden
    b. Making Tomato Juice
    c. Drinking Tomato Juice

B. Read the sentences below. One of them does not tell about the same subject that the other three do. Write in paragraph form the three sentences which tell about one subject. Remember to write them in the correct order.

1. Kathy and I folded them neatly.
2. Our dog, Rags, caught a groundhog.
3. Mary took the dry clothes off the line.
4. Then we put them away in the drawers.

Review Two

⊃ Oral Drill ⊃

A. Telling about what we see, hear, and feel:

   1. Use a sentence to describe how each thing named below might look.

      a. snow   b. a rooster
      c. a lamb   d. a truck

   2. Use a sentence to describe how each thing above might sound.

   3. Use a sentence to describe how each thing above might feel.

B. Use a rhyming word to complete each poem below.

   1. Father said that he would wait
      Until I shut the pasture ——.

   2. I saw a rainbow in the sky.
      It made me think of God on ——.

   3. The little birds sang merrily,
      Sitting in the apple ——.

   4. We know that it might soon be snowing
      When we hear the cold wind ——.

> **Written Practice** >

A. Read each sentence below carefully. On your paper write whether the sentence helps you see, hear, or feel what is being described. Some sentences have more than one answer.

1. The little, yellow ducklings splashed in the water.
2. The hail clattered loudly on the roof.
3. Mother sang as she folded the soft, white towels.
4. The blackberry bushes scratched our hands.
5. The two boys laughed as they brushed the wet snow off their coats.

B. Use a number word to make each poem below rhyme. Write each poem correctly.

1. I saw some kittens on the floor.
   I counted them, and there were ——.
2. Some birds were perched upon our gate.
   I counted them, and there were ——.
3. Some bees were buzzing by the hive.
   I counted them, and there were ——.

Extra Activity

Making A Poem Book

Copy neatly the five poems found at the end of the first five units in your English book. Write each poem on a separate sheet of clean, white paper.

Trim around the poems to cut off the extra paper. Then paste the poems onto colorful construction paper. Put pictures or seals around each poem.

Put the pages together to form a book. Maybe you will want to give the book to somebody who is not always able to go to church.

A Poem to Enjoy

A Smile, A Word

Something each day—a smile,
  It is not much to give,
And the little gifts of life
  Make sweeter the days we live.
The world has weary hearts
  That we can bless and cheer,
And a smile for every day
  Makes sunshine all the year.

—William Wiseman

Discussing the poem:

1. What does the poem say we can give?
2. How often can we give one?
3. Is it a big gift, or a little gift?
4. How does the gift help the people to whom we give it?

Unit VI

Building Our Vocabulary

"Set a watch, O Lord, before my mouth; keep the door of my lips."

Psalm 141:3

1. Alphabetical Order

Say the twenty-six letters of the alphabet. Did you say them in order from **A** to **Z**? If you said the letters in correct order from **A** to **Z**, you said them in **alphabetical** (al′fə•bet′i•kəl) order.

Sometimes we put words in alphabetical order. When we do this, we write them in the order in which their first letters come in the alphabet. This means that all the words which begin with the letter a̲ come first, then the words which begin with the letter b̲, and so on.

Look at the groups of words below. The words in each list are written in alphabetical order.

a̲pple	f̲ather	l̲ate	r̲ide
b̲read	g̲reat	m̲uch	s̲low
c̲ousin	h̲appy	n̲oun	t̲eacher

To write words in alphabetical order, look at the first letter of each word. Then write the words in the same order as their first letters come in the alphabet.

> **Class Practice** >

A. Find the dictionary at the back of this book. Look for the words that begin with the letter **a**. They will be found at the beginning of the dictionary. Then find the words which begin with **b**, **c**, **d**, etc.

B. Read each group of words below. Say the words in each group in alphabetical order.

1.	bark	3.	early	5.	ink	7.	jam
	crow		faith		hope		life
	able		door		give		keep
2.	open	4.	trust	6.	van	8.	yellow
	more		rest		use		zebra
	none		quiet		wait		x-ray
	pray		stay				

> **For You to Do** >

A. Write the alphabet neatly on your paper. Check to be certain that you have written all the letters in correct order.

B. Write the words in each group below in alphabetical order.

1.	break	2.	cord	3.	play	4.	upon	5.	gray
	crack		east		move		stop		iron
	attic		five		oxen		trip		floor
	drive		dive		need		read		hide

2. More Work With Alphabetical Order

When we want to write words in alphabetical order, we first look at the first letter in each word. Look at the first letter of each word in each list below. Are the words written in alphabetical order?

1. apron	2. all	3. age	4. ache
berry	cow	bow	comb
cloud	dew	den	echo
dust	end	eat	fast

The first word in each list above begins with the letter **a**. In group 1, the first letters of the words are **a-b-c-d**. When we say the alphabet, we say **a-b-c-d**.

In group 2, the first letters are **a-c-d-e**. There is no word in group 2 which begins with the letter *b*, but the words are still in alphabetical order. They are in alphabetical order because the words are written in the order in which their first letters come in the alphabet.

Look at groups 3 and 4. The words in these groups are in alphabetical order also. Can you tell what letters have been skipped in each group?

DIANE   BARBARA   ANITA   CLAIR

> Class Practice >

Say the words in each group below in alphabetical order.

1. brown	3. dry	5. son	7. part
earth	hen	win	keep
angel	cat	ten	meat
crown	few	run	oven
2. clap	4. giant	6. queen	8. trade
door	James	lamp	water
away	inside	offer	slide
east	floor	many	under

> For You to Do >

A. One word is missing from each list below. Choose a word from the box to complete each list. Be sure to choose a word which will keep the list in alphabetical order. Write each list correctly.

1. ——	3. dry	5. glove	7. Kathy
brown	edge	——	later
cake	——	ice	——
done	goat	John	none
2. nine	4. quilt	6. town	8. water
——	round	use	Xerxes
pearl	——	——	year
quiet	treat	went	——

few	mine	vine	heard
store	aunt	zero	often

3. More Alphabet Practice

Our alphabet has twenty-six letters. Each letter has its own special place where it belongs in the alphabet. To be able to put words in alphabetical order, you must know well exactly where each letter comes in the alphabet. Here are some practice drills for you to do.

A. Say the letters in each group in the order in which they come in the alphabet.

1. b-c-a-f-d   6. h-a-f-m-d   11. a-q-h-z
2. k-a-c-d-g   7. t-x-r-p-v   12. t-l-d-p
3. l-o-r-t-m   8. i-b-g-j-e   13. g-s-b-y
4. y-w-x-v-z   9. q-n-p-s-l   14. c-p-i-w
5. i-f-h-j-k   10. h-e-c-j-f   15. e-v-j-f

B. We can divide the alphabet into three sections:

A-H   I-Q   R-Z

Read each word below, and then tell by looking at the first letter in each word in which section of the alphabet each word would belong.

1. ready   5. well   9. fire   13. count
2. hard   6. June   10. stop   14. past
3. quit   7. grace   11. lost   15. uncle
4. blue   8. need   12. twin   16. king

> Class Practice >

A. Say the words in each group below in alphabetical order. Then say how the words in each group are related.

1. bees	2. orange	3. carrots	4. Ruth
moths	melon	beans	Alice
ants	peach	squash	Carol
fleas	banana	onions	Mary
wasps	lemon	peas	Tina

B. Say the words in each list below in alphabetical order.

1. promises   Abraham   God's   believed

2. donkey   spoke   Balaam's

3. Zebedee   spoke   a   to   man

4. good   angels   news   brought

5. shone   light   a   bright

> For You to Do >

A. Write the words in each group below in alphabetical order.

1. come	2. trip	3. get	4. light
ask	poem	mice	right
beg	used	like	sight
eat	rest	have	might
give	nest	dust	tight

B. In alphabetical order write the names of five boys you know.

4. When Words Begin With the Same Letters

You learned how to put words in alphabetical order when each word begins with a different letter. But many words begin with the same letters. Look at the words below. How would we put them in alphabetical order?

added   able   after   action   again

When two or more words begin with the same letters, we must look at the second letter in each word. In the words above, the second letters are **d-b-f-c-g**. To write these letters in alphabetical order, we would write **b-c-d-f-g**. To write the above words in alphabetical order, we would write them in the same order as their **second** letters come in the alphabet.

able   action   added   after   again

Look at the lists of words below. In each list the first letters of the words are the same, but the second letters are different.

black	camel	shore	wash
bound	chair	sing	whale
bring	cover	skill	with
butter	crown	story	woman

The words in each list above are in alphabetical order. They are written in the order in which their second letters come in the alphabet.

> Class Practice >

Say the words in each list in alphabetical order.

1. bite	3. does	5. echo	7. pillow
bead	damp	each	please
blow	dial	ebony	power
bang	desk	edge	phrase
2. hurt	4. geese	6. sour	8. fly
hour	guest	small	fell
hill	greet	snow	foam
head	gave	spot	five

> For You to Do >

A. Write each list in alphabetical order.

1. pen	2. cot	3. say	4. try
pin	cat	sit	toe
pry	cut	sun	two
pan	chat	sob	the

B. Choose a word from the box to complete each list below, keeping each list in alphabetical order. Write each list correctly.

cover	after	ark	cereal

1. —	2. cave	3. chair	4. act
again	—	close	age
asleep	church	—	—
awake	city	create	ask

5. More Practice With Alphabetical Order

Charles   Barry   Carol   Steven   Karen

Look at the five names at the top of this page. How would you put the names in alphabetical order? Some of them begin with different letters, and some of them begin with the same letters.

Since none of the names begins with **a**, we must find the name that begins with the letter closest to **a**. The name **Barry** begins with **b**. **Barry** should come first in alphabetical order.

Do any names begin with **c**? **Charles** and **Carol** both begin with **c**. Since more than one name begins with **c**, we must look at their second letters. Which letter comes first, **h** or **a**? **A** comes before **h**, so we should write **Carol** before **Charles**.

Now look at the last two names in the list. Which name should come after **Charles**? Which should come last?

This is how the names should be written in alphabetical order:

Barry   Carol   Charles   Karen   Steven

> Class Practice >

Say the words in each list in alphabetical order.

1. cart   blew   drop   big   find
2. hard   help   easy   hurt   keep

3. sing   read   page   ride   said

4. bake   like   lock   take   lake

5. dress   elbow   down   earn   dark

> **For You to Do**

A. Write these headings on your paper:

Colors   Sizes   Animals   People

Decide which list belongs with each heading. Write each list under the correct heading in alphabetical order.

1. dogs	2. small	3. son	4. yellow
cows	large	brother	black
skunks	little	father	pink
cats	tiny	aunt	green
lions	big	friend	brown
seals	huge	sister	purple

B. Write the words in each group below in alphabetical order. If they are written correctly they will make a sentence.

1. might   many   move   men

2. yellow   vases   two   were   the

3. wagon   the   Douglas   drive   did

4. roses   picked   pretty   Paula

5. Simeon   smile   see   Sarah   did

6. the   hidden   whistle   Henry   has

7. to   Brian   Uncle   crawled   Baby   William

6. When the First Two Letters Are the Same

You have learned how to put words into alphabetical order when the words begin with different letters. You have also learned how to put them in order when they begin with the same letters but have different second letters.

Sometimes two or more words have the same first and second letters. When words have the same first and second letters, we must look at the **third** letter in each word to know how to put the words in alphabetical order.

Look at each list of words below. The words in each list have the same first and second letters, but their third letters are different. The words in each list have been put in alphabetical order by writing the words in the order in which their third letters come in the alphabet.

bi<u>b</u>	sa<u>d</u>	ho<u>e</u>	ma<u>n</u>	pe<u>g</u>	ru<u>b</u>
bi<u>d</u>	sa<u>g</u>	ho<u>g</u>	ma<u>p</u>	pe<u>n</u>	ru<u>g</u>
bi<u>g</u>	sa<u>t</u>	ho<u>p</u>	ma<u>t</u>	pe<u>t</u>	ru<u>n</u>
bi<u>t</u>	sa<u>y</u>	ho<u>t</u>	ma<u>y</u>	pe<u>w</u>	ru<u>t</u>

Now try to put the five words below in alphabetical order. Since each word begins with the letters **ca** you will need to look at the third letter in each word.

can   car   cap   cat   cab

> Class Practice >

Say the words in each list in alphabetical order.

1. hat	3. box	5. tag	7. toy
ham	bow	tab	ton
has	bog	tan	toe
had	boy	tar	top
2. bend	4. done	6. star	8. dips
best	dome	stub	dial
belt	doll	stop	dirt
bead	door	stir	dill

> For You to Do >

Write the words in each list in alphabetical order.
Draw a line under the third letter in each word.

1. beg	3. Pam	5. sow	7. cud
Ben	pat	sob	cut
bed	pay	son	cub
bee	pan	sod	cue
2. whip	4. find	6. sore	8. quite
when	figs	soup	quail
what	fire	sobs	quote
whose	fill	soap	queen

7. Using Alphabetical Order

Alphabetical order is used to help us find words and names quickly. A dictionary has many words in it. If the words were not in alphabetical order, we would have to spend much time looking for any word we wanted to find.

Alphabetical order is not used only in a dictionary. The **index** in a song book is another place where alphabetical order is used. The index lists all the songs which are in the book.

Find the index at the back of a song book. Can you find the songs which begin with the letter **A**? Perhaps some of these songs are listed in the index:

> **Abide With Me**
> **All Hail the Power of Jesus' Name**
> **Amazing Grace**
> **Away in a Manger**

Look at the first word in the title of each song named above. Each of the first words begins with the letter **A**. The second letters are **b-l-m-w**. These letters are in the same order as they come in the alphabet. The song titles in the list above are written in alphabetical order.

> **Class Activity** >

Your teacher will write on the board the title of a song. Tell what letter the title begins with. Find the section of the index which lists the songs that begin with this same letter. Then look at the second letter in the title. Use alphabetical order to help you find the song.

What number comes after the title in the index? This number tells you where you will find the song in the book.

> **For You to Do** >

A. Write the words in each group in alphabetical order.

1. east	2. cone	3. acts	4. rain
ears	crow	bear	pour
each	claw	able	rake
eats	cage	star	leaf

B. Write the words in each list below in alphabetical order. Then tell how the words in each list are related.

1. house   barn   shed   store   school
2. lily   rose   poppy   daisy   daffodil
3. March   April   May   June   July

C. See if you can find these songs in an index. Write the page number which tells where each song is found in the book.

Take Time to Be Holy
More About Jesus

8. Writing Names in Alphabetical Order

Your teacher probably has a **roll book**. He uses the roll book to keep a record of each pupil's grades. Every pupil's name is in the roll book. Usually the names are written in alphabetical order. By writing the names in alphabetical order, the teacher is able to quickly find the name of each pupil.

A **telephone book** is another book in which the names are written in alphabetical order. Many people's names are in the telephone book. Without alphabetical order it would be very difficult to find a name in the telephone book.

When we want to write names in alphabetical order, we must write each person's last name first. We put a comma between the last and first names.

> Kevin Gray ⟶ Gray, Kevin
> Mary Jones ⟶ Jones, Mary
> Howard White ⟶ White, Howard

Look in a telephone book. You will see that all the names are written with the person's last name first. Then the last names are written in alphabetical order.

> **For You to Do** >

A. Write the names in each list below in alphabetical order. Remember to write each person's last name first.

1. Carl Green
   Daniel Bates
   Timothy Hunt
   Jason Jones

2. Jane Weber
   Susan Nolt
   Rita Martin
   Lois Smith

B. Write in alphabetical order the names of five people in your classroom.

> **More Practice and Review** >

Choose a word from the box to complete each list below. Use a word which will keep the list in alphabetical order. Write each list correctly.

sews	soda	safe	side

1. ——
   save
   scar
   seal

2. seed
   send
   ——
   shed

3. shop
   ——
   sing
   sips

4. skip
   slow
   snow
   ——

9. More Practice Writing Names in Alphabetical Order

You have learned how to write names in alphabetical order when each person has a different last name. But what do we do when two or more people have the same last name?

Weaver, Charles
Weaver, Mary
Weaver, Ruth

Each person named above has the last name **Weaver**. To write these names in alphabetical order we must look at each person's first name. The first names begin with the letters **C-M-R**. These names are written in alphabetical order because they are written in the same order as their first letters come in the alphabet.

Look at each list below. The names in each list are written in alphabetical order. Since the last names in each list are the same, we looked at the first name of each person to know how to write the names in alphabetical order.

Powers, Amy   Rogers, Miriam
Powers, David   Rogers, Paul
Powers, Earl   Rogers, Peter
Powers, George   Rogers, Susan

> Class Practice >

Say the names in each list in alphabetical order.

1. Jones, Martha 2. Smith, Laura
   Jones, Alice   Smith, Brenda
   Jones, Terry   Smith, Brian
   Jones, Carol   Smith, Barbara
   Jones, Ruth   Smith, David

◇ For You to Do ◇

A. Write the names in each list in alphabetical order.

1. Karen Williams 2. Nancy Mast
   Lisa White   Lois Mast
   Susan Green   Kathy Mast
   Janet King   Irene Mast

B. For each word below, write a word which would come before that word in alphabetical order. Then write another word which would come after the given word in alphabetical order.

1. ——bread——
2. ——drive——
3. ——awake——
4. ——many——
5. ——very——

10. Reviewing Alphabetical Order

> ▷ **Class Practice** ▷

A. Say the words in each list in alphabetical order. Then tell how the words in each list are related.

1. willow	2. robin	3. two	4. sleet
birch	wren	three	hail
maple	sparrow	ten	snow
elm	bobwhite	twenty	rain
oak	starling	thirteen	fog

B. Say these song titles in alphabetical order. How many of the songs can you find in your song book?

What a Friend We Have in Jesus
Awake My Soul
Savior, Like a Shepherd Lead Us
Walking in Sunlight
My Hope Is Built on Nothing Less

C. Say in correct alphabetical order the names of the pupils in your classroom. Each pupil should write his or her name on the board as it is said. Remember to write your last name first and to use a comma between your last name and first name.

> **For You to Do** >

A. On your paper write the word or words which correctly complete each sentence below. Take time to spell each word correctly.

1. — order helps us find words quickly.
2. Alphabetical order is used in a —, in the — of a song book, in a teacher's — book, and in a — book.
3. When we write words in alphabetical order, we first look at the — letter of each word.
4. We write the words in the same order as their first letters come in the —.
5. When we write names in alphabetical order, we must write each person's — name first.

B. Write the words or names in each list in alphabetical order.

1. hard	2. play	3. Nancy Brown
soft	wash	Keith Stoner
happy	work	Lester Amber
great	ring	Simon Drake
quiet	keep	Anne Martin

11. Meeting the Dictionary

Many books have been written to help us know special things. God gave us the Bible to help us know about Him and His will for us. The Bible tells us the most important things we need to know.

Man has written books to help us in other ways. Your English book has been written to help you learn to speak and write correctly. Your English book teaches you about the English language. A **dictionary** teaches you about the English language also. A dictionary teaches you about the words you use to speak and write.

Many words are found in a dictionary. The words in a dictionary are all written in alphabetical order. We can divide a dictionary into three parts. The first part lists the words which begin with the letters **A-H**. The middle part lists the words which begin with the letters **I-Q**. The last part of the dictionary lists the words which begin with the letters **R-Z**.

Look at each word below. Tell whether you would find the word in the **front, middle,** or **back** of a dictionary.

camel	smile	friend	plenty
rest	dream	holy	white
glory	long	train	early

> Class Practice

A. Turn to the dictionary at the back of this book. Find the words which begin with the letter **a.** What is the first word which is listed? What is the last word which is listed that begins with the letter **a**? How many words in this dictionary begin with the letter **a**?

B. Tell on which page we would find the last word that begins with:

f   h   l   o   r   w

> For You to Do >

A. Use the dictionary at the back of this book to answer these questions:

1. What is the first word listed that begins with **b**? with **c**? with **d**?

2. What is the last word listed in the dictionary? With what letter does this word begin?

B. Tell whether each word below would be found in the **front, middle,** or **back** of a dictionary.

ready	apple	store	leave
broad	praise	earn	voice

12. Finding Correct Pronunciations

A dictionary gives us much helpful information about words. When we want to know how to spell a word, we can check a dictionary. When we want to know the meaning of a word, we can check a dictionary. We can also check a dictionary when we want to know how to pronounce a word correctly.

Find the first word listed under the letter **a** in the dictionary at the back of this book. The word is **accurate.** First we find the correct way to spell the word. Then we find the correct **pronunciation** (pr ə •nun′sē•ā′shən) of the word. The pronunciation of the word is written in **parentheses** ( ): (ak′yər•it).

Now look at the page opposite the beginning of the dictionary. There you will find the **pronunciation key.** The **pronunciation key** tells you which letters and symbols are used to stand for different sounds. Use this pronunciation key and what you have learned about phonics in your reading classes to help you sound out the correct pronunciation of the word **accurate.**

Probably, when you are reading, you sometimes find words which you do not know how to pronounce correctly. Learn to use a dictionary to find the correct way to pronounce any words you do not know.

> ▷ Class Practice ▷

A. The words listed below are found in the Bible or

in familiar hymns. Find each word in the dictionary and practice saying each word correctly.

1. brethren   3. aught   5. tumult
2. incarnate   4. grievous   6. countenance

B. Read carefully each pronunciation given below. Can you spell each word correctly?

1. ə•līv′   4. klīm   7. kum
2. sez   5. lo͞os   8. tro͞o
3. prit′ē   6. lo͞oz   9. kwī′ət

> For You to Do >

A. Find each of the words below in the dictionary. Write the correct pronunciation on your paper. Learn to say each word correctly.

1. genuine   2. dessert   3. complete

B. Written below are three sentences, but the words in each sentence are written the way they are pronounced. Sound out each word, and then write each sentence correctly.

1. thə bī′bəl iz godz wûrd
2. wē sho͝od ō•bā′ our pâr′ənts
3. jē′zəs chōz twelv di•sī′pəls

13. Finding Word Meanings

When you are reading, you probably find some words that you do not understand. What do you do? When you do not know the meaning of a word, you should learn to look in a dictionary. The dictionary will tell you what the word means. Read the meaning of the word carefully. Think about what the word means. Then try to use the word in a sentence.

Read the sentence below.

Kathy visited a **zoological** park.

Do you know what the word in bold print means? Find the word in your dictionary. Read the pronunciation of the word carefully. Notice that the first syllable is pronounced zō. Then read the meaning of the word.

Does what the dictionary says the word means help you understand what kind of park Kathy visited? She visited a park where animals are kept. If you have ever been to a **zoo**, you have been to a **zoological park**. Actually, a **zoological park** is the full name for a **zoo**.

> Class Practice >

A. Find the words below in your dictionary. Pronounce each word correctly. Then read the meaning of each word. Take turns using the words in sentences.

   1. blind   2. deaf   3. lame

B. Each of the words below begins with the letters *ea*. Find each word in the dictionary, and say each one correctly. Then use each word in a sentence.

   1. easy   2. ear   3. early

> For You to Do >

A. Find each of the words below in your dictionary. On your paper write the correct pronunciation of each word. Read the meaning of each word carefully.

   1. omnipotent   2. impotent   3. potent

B. Use one of the above words to complete each sentence below. Write each sentence correctly.

   1. The —— man could not walk.

   2. Only God is truly ——.

   3. The doctor gave Lois a —— medicine.

C. Write three sentences using three of the words you learned in Class Practice.

14. More Practice Finding Definitions

Do you know what a definition is? Find the word **definition** in the dictionary. The dictionary tells you that a **definition** is the meaning of a word. When we use a dictionary to find a word's meaning, we are finding the **definition** of the word.

Our English language has many words. None of us know all the words in our language. Each of us has to sometimes use a dictionary to find the meaning of a word which we do not know. As we learn to know the meanings of more and more words, our **vocabulary** grows.

Do you know what your **vocabulary** is? Find the word **vocabulary** in the dictionary. The dictionary tells you that a **vocabulary** is a list of words, or a list of all the words which a person knows and uses. So, by learning to know and to use more words, you make your vocabulary grow.

> **Class Practice**

Find the words below in your dictionary. Read each definition carefully. Take turns using the words in sentences.

1. wild　　2. tame　　3. aid

▷ For You to Do ▷

A. Write the words below on your paper. Find each word in the dictionary. Next to each word write its pronunciation. Then read the meaning of each word carefully.

   1. ache   3. doze   5. polite

   2. indigo   4. burro   6. neigh

B. Copy the sentences below, using one of the words above to complete each sentence correctly.

   1. We should be —— to everyone.

   2. The man placed a saddle on the back of his ——.

   3. Grandmother was sleepy and began to —— in her rocking chair.

   4. The horse gave a loud ——.

   5. John's knees —— where he bruised them.

   6. The early morning sky was the color of ——.

15. Words Used in the Bible

Read the five words given below. Can you say what each word means?

cubit   span   astray   stature   famine

Each of the words above is used in the Bible. It would be difficult to understand some verses in the Bible if you did not know what these words mean. In 1 Samuel 17:4 the words **cubit** and **span** are used to tell us how tall Goliath was.

". . . Goliath, of Gath, whose height was
six **cubits** and a **span**."

Many years ago when people measured something, they used **cubits** and **spans**, just as we use **feet** and **inches** today. Find the words **cubit** and **span** in the dictionary. Read the definition of each word. How long is a **cubit**? How long is a **span**? Can you figure out how tall Goliath was? We could say that he was **9 feet 9 inches** tall. Most men that you know are probably only about **6 feet** tall!

Learn to use a dictionary when you do not understand a word which you read in the Bible. If you learn to check word meanings, you will be better able to understand what God is saying in His Word.

> Class Practice

Find the words **astray**, **stature**, and **famine** in the dictionary. Then find the verses given below in your Bible. Discuss what each verse means.

Genesis 41:57   Matthew 18:12

Luke 2:52   Luke 12:25

> For You to Do >

Find each of the words in bold print in your dictionary. Write the word and its meaning on your paper. Then think carefully about each verse and be ready to discuss in class what each verse means.

1. "Blessed are the **meek**." (Matthew 5:5)

2. "Take heed that ye do not your **alms** before men." (Matthew 6:1)

3. "Is not the life more than meat, and the body than **raiment**?" (Matthew 6:25)

4. "I cried to thee, O Lord; and unto the Lord I made **supplication**." (Psalm 30:8)

5. "Fear not ye: for I know that ye **seek** Jesus, which was crucified." (Matthew 28:5)

16. Words That Sound the Same

Our English language has some words which sound the same but are spelled differently. Read the pairs of words below. What is unusual about the words in each pair?

| some | knew | pair | wait |
| sum | new | pear | weight |

The words in each pair sound the same. The words are not spelled the same, and they do not mean the same thing. But still they sound the same.

Can you use each of the words above correctly in a sentence?

> **Class Practice**

Find the words given below in your dictionary. Look at the pronunciation of each word. Are the two words in each pair pronounced the same? Read the definition of each word. Use each word correctly in a sentence.

1. hear—here   3. flee—flea
2. hare—hair   4. tale—tail

> **For You to Do**

A. Copy the pairs of words given below. Next to each word write the correct definition from the list. Use the dictionary if you need help.

1. pair   a. seven days
   pear   b. look with the eyes

2. inn   c. the opposite of out

   in   d. a body of water

3. weak   e. two of a kind

   week   f. not strong

4. see   g. single

   sea   h. a type of fruit

5. won   i. a place for people to eat

   one   j. did not lose

B. Look at the pictures below. Read the pair of words written below each picture. On your paper write the correct word from each pair to name what is shown in the picture. Use your dictionary if you need help.

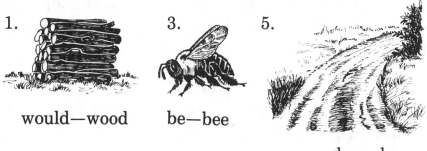

1. would—wood

3. be—bee

5. road—rode

2. meat—meet

4. sale—sail

6. deer—dear

17. More Words Which Sound the Same

Read the two sentences below. Can you think of a word which you could use to complete the second sentence which sounds the same as a word used in the first sentence?

Janet is eight years old.
The horses —— the hay.

Say the words in the first sentence carefully. Is there one of them that sounds the same as a word which you could use to complete the second sentence? Say the word **eight**. Is there another word you know which sounds the same? The words **eight** and **ate** sound alike. We could use the word **ate** to complete the second sentence.

The horses **ate** the hay.

When you write words, you must be careful to spell each word correctly. If there are two words that sound the same, be careful to spell the word which you actually want to use.

Read the two sentences below. In which sentence would you use the word **blew**? In which one would you use **blue**?

The sky today is bright ——.
The wind —— through the trees.

> For You to Do

Fill in the blank in the second sentence in each pair

with a word which sounds like a word used in the first sentence. Write the second sentence of each pair correctly.

1. a. Jacob was Isaac's son.
   b. God made the ——, moon, and stars.

2. a. Wear your rubbers to the barn.
   b. A bicycle has —— wheels.

3. a. It was raining so hard yesterday.
   b. Mother taught Amy how to —— a dress.

4. a. No children are absent today.
   b. Do you —— how to multiply?

5. a. In the winter many trees are bare.
   b. We saw a black —— at the park.

6. a. This book is for Susan to read.
   b. Our cat has —— new kittens.

7. a. Mother read us a story.
   b. Our cousins have a —— wagon.

8. a. A penny is worth one cent.
   b. Mother —— Aunt Rhoda a letter.

9. a. Would you please help me?
   b. The boys stacked the ——.

10. a. Jonah tried to flee from God.
    b. A —— is a tiny, black insect.

18. Words That Mean the Same

What does **big** mean? What does **large** mean? Read the two sentences below. Do they mean the same thing?

This chair is **big**.
This chair is **large**.

Big and **large** are two words that mean about the same thing. Read the pairs of words below. The words in each pair mean the same or nearly the same thing.

little	happy	kind	fix
small	glad	gentle	repair

A dictionary definition of a word often tells us other words that have the same meaning. Find the word **frighten** in your dictionary. The first part of the definition tells us that **frighten** means **to make afraid**. The second part of the definition uses the word **scare**. The words **frighten** and **scare** mean about the same thing.

> Class Practice >

Say a word with nearly the same meaning for each word below. Use the dictionary if you need help.

1. neat   3. sober   5. sick
2. shy   4. talk   6. enough

> For You to Do >

A. Match the words which mean the same or nearly the same. Write the words in pairs. Use your dictionary if you need help.

1. seek   a. hurt
2. cold   b. like
3. enjoy   c. look for
4. ache   d. chilly

B. Use one of the words from part A above to complete each sentence below. Write each sentence correctly.

1. Does your tooth ——?
2. The weather this morning is ——.
3. The boys —— playing ball.
4. The shepherd will —— the lost lamb.

19. Using Words That Mean the Same

Sometimes we use different words that mean the same or nearly the same to give our writing more variety. That way we do not need to use the same words over and over again. Read the two sentences below.

> The **little** girl found a **little** kitten under the **little** bush.
> The **little** girl found a **tiny** kitten under the **small** bush.

The first sentence uses the word **little** three times. The second sentence uses the words **little, tiny,** and **small. Little, tiny,** and **small** mean nearly the same. Using these words gives the second sentence variety.

In the sentences below, the words in bold print mean nearly the same. The different words are used to give more variety to each sentence.

> Kathy is a **cheerful** girl and always has a **happy** smile.
> On our walk we saw many **pretty** flowers and **beautiful** trees.
> Luke's hands were **clean** and his face was **spotless.**

> **Class Practice** >

Sometimes people who come from different places use different words for the same thing. Match each word in the first list with one from the second list which names the same thing. Which words do you usually use?

List A   List B

List A		List B	
seesaw	couch	stream	tap
creek	bag	bucket	sofa
faucet	pail	sack	teeter-totter

> **For You to Do** >

Rewrite each sentence, changing the word in bold print to another word which means nearly the same thing. Use the list below to help you. If you do not understand a word, check your dictionary.

1. The dog's barking **scared** Kathy.
2. Did you **finish** your work?
3. Children should **respect** their parents.
4. Carl is a **courteous** boy.
5. Samuel **tripped** over the log.
6. Karen was **sad** when her kitten died.

    polite   **sorrowful**   **complete**
    honor   **frightened**   **stumbled**

20. Choosing More Exact Words

By choosing our words carefully, we can say more accurately what we mean. Read these two sentences:

> An elephant is a **big** animal.
> An elephant is a **huge** animal.

Many animals are big. A bear is big, but it is not as big as an elephant. An elephant is very big. **Huge** means **very big**. The word **huge** helps us describe an elephant more accurately.

Read the pairs of sentences below. Notice how the word in bold print helps the second sentence in each pair say more accurately what is meant.

> The monkeys at the zoo talked loudly.
> The monkeys at the zoo **chattered** loudly.

> We watched the ducks walk to the pond.
> We watched the ducks **waddle** to the pond.

> The men spread more stones over the lane.
> The men spread more **gravel** over the lane.

When you write, choose words which will help you say accurately what you mean. Use different words to make your writing more interesting and exact.

> **For You to Do** >

A. Decide which word best completes each sentence below. Write the words on your paper. Use your dictionary if you need help.

1. hit—knock
   a. Please —— on the door before entering.
   b. Can you —— the tree with that ball?

2. ran—galloped
   a. The water —— down the rain gutter.
   b. The horses —— across the field.

3. smiled—grinned
   a. Mother —— happily at the children.
   b. Tom and Isaac —— at each other.

4. walk—strut
   a. Our rooster likes to —— around the barnyard.
   b. I saw Father —— to the barn.

5. drink—sip
   a. May I please have a cold —— of water?
   b. Take a tiny —— through the straw.

B. Find each of the words below in your dictionary. Then use each word in a sentence.

1. draw   2. sketch   3. sleep   4. nap

21. More Practice Choosing Exact Words

When we speak and write, we should try to use words which say exactly what we mean. We could say: The horse **made a noise.**

Can you think of a more accurate way to say what noise the horse made?

The horse **neighed.**

Most animals make some noise, but they do not all make the same kind of noise. The word **neigh** tells us what kind of noise a horse makes. What kind of noise does a mouse make? What kind of noise does a lion make? We can say that a mouse **squeaks** and a lion **roars.**

We can choose exact words to describe the different ways that things move also. We can say that a snake **slithers.** A rooster **struts,** and a mouse **scurries.** A child might **skip** or **hop.**

When you write and speak, remember to use words which say exactly what you mean. Train your mind to work and to think of words which will make your writing and speaking more interesting for others to read and hear.

> Class Practice >

A. Find the words below in the dictionary. How many animals can you think of that make each sound?

1. peep   3. buzz   5. chirp
2. squawk   4. purr   6. howl

B. The three words below name three different types of storms. Find the words in your dictionary. Discuss in class how each storm is different.

1. blizzard   2. hurricane   3. sandstorm

> For You to Do >

A. Write these five words on your paper:

1. wash   2. sleep   3. walk   4. look   5. push

After each word write the letter of the list below which tells different ways which we might do each thing.

a. watch, stare, glance
b. hike, march, stroll
c. scrub, scour, mop
d. shove, press, nudge
e. nap, doze, slumber

B. Write five sentences. Use one word from each list above.

22. Words Which Tell How We Move

Different animals move in different ways. A snake slithers, and a rooster struts. A duck waddles, and a snail crawls.

People have different ways of moving or walking, also. Here are some words which name different ways that people might move:

limp   stroll   dash   skip   tiptoe

A person with a hurt foot might **limp**. Someone who is taking a walk might **stroll**. A boy in a hurry might **dash** out the door. A girl might **skip** happily. Someone who wants to be very quiet might **tiptoe**.

Using different words to tell how people move adds variety to our sentences. Words such as **limp** and **dash** help us have more exact pictures in our minds of what is happening. Practice using exact words to describe how people move.

> **Class Practice**

Take turns showing how a person might **limp, stroll, dash, skip,** or **tiptoe.** Then use one of the words to complete each of the following sentences correctly.

1. Mother asked us to —— while Grandfather was sleeping.

2. We saw Mr. Green —— painfully down the lane.

3. In the evening, my grandparents like to —— through the meadow.

4. When the boys saw the bull, they decided to —— to the fence.

5. Aunt Eva watched Alice —— happily to the car.

> For You to Do >

A. The words below name other ways that people might move. Match each word with its definition by writing the word and the correct letter together on your paper. Use your dictionary if you need help.

1. jump   a. to move on the hands and knees

2. hop   b. to walk slowly with a limp

3. hobble   c. to move very quickly

4. crawl   d. to spring from the ground with
5. run   one foot

            e. to spring from the ground with
               both feet

B. Write three sentences telling about someone moving. Use three of the words from part A above.

23. Words That Are Opposites

God has made the world in a wonderful way. He has made the day, and He has made the night. In the day it is light. In the night it is dark. God has made the different seasons. Sometimes it is hot, and sometimes it is cold. Sometimes it is wet, and sometimes it is dry.

God has made the world so that it is not the same all the time. God has made many opposites in the world. **Day** and **night** are opposites. **Light** and **dark** are opposites. Read the words below. The words in each pair are opposites.

hot—cold   big—little   quiet—loud
high—low   love—hate   seek—lose

> Class Practice >

Match each word below with its opposite.

1. large	9. sinful	a. tall	i. boy
2. tiny	10. black	b. frown	j. big
3. never	11. dry	c. sick	k. old
4. happy	12. stop	d. holy	l. whisper
5. short	13. smile	e. go	m. bad
6. narrow	14. shout	f. white	n. wet
7. good	15. young	g. small	o. always
8. girl	16. healthy	h. wide	p. sad

> For You to Do >

A. Match each word below with its opposite.

1. cried   **happy**

2. sad   **awake**

3. wild   **mend**

4. away   **laughed**

5. asleep   **tight**

6. tear   **tame**

7. lose   **find**

8. loose   **toward**

B. Write five sentences. Use at least one of the above words in each sentence. If you can, use two of the above words in a sentence together.

Example: The **wild** animals ran **away** from us.

☆ Some verses in the Bible talk about opposites. Ecclesiastes 3:2-8 is a familiar passage which talks about opposites. Read these verses in your Bible. Make a list of as many opposites as you can find in these verses.

24. Practice With Opposites

You have been learning new words to add to your vocabulary. You have to use your mind to remember the new words which you have learned. You have to use your mind to think of the best word to use to say what you want to say.

Learning opposites helps your vocabulary grow also. Learning to use opposites will help you to add variety to your sentences. Read the two sentences below.

The large chair is heavy, but the chair which is not large is not heavy.
The large chair is heavy, but the small chair is light.

In the first sentence above, the words **large** and **heavy** are used twice. The second sentence says the same thing as the first sentence but uses different words. The second sentence uses the words **small** and **light** to mean the opposite of **large** and **heavy**. The second sentence is written more simply and with more variety.

Remember to use opposites when you write. Use opposites to help you say clearly, exactly what you mean. Make your mind work to think of the best word to use to say what you want to say.

> Class Practice >

Answer each question below with a complete sentence. Make your sentence say the opposite.

Example: Is the weather **warm**?
No, it is **cool**.

1. Is the plate **clean**?
2. Is the knife **dull**?
3. Is that tree **dead**?
4. Is that tomato **ripe**?
5. Is that couch **soft**?
6. Were you **careless**?
7. Is your work **easy**?
8. Are you **sick**?
9. Are you **playing**?
10. Is the cup **empty**?

> For You to Do >

A. Copy each word below. Next to each word write another word which means the opposite.

1. hard
2. rough
3. humble
4. cruel
5. under
6. out
7. on
8. dirty
9. open

B. Write two sentences about each picture below. Use words which are opposites to tell about the two things you see in each picture.

1.

2.

25. Reviewing What We Have Learned

A. You have learned that some words sound the same, but are spelled differently and have different meanings. Complete the second sentence in each pair below with a word which sounds like a word that is used in the first sentence. Write the word that you use to complete the second sentence.

1. James knew the answer.
   Janet has —— shoes.
2. Father saw a hare in the pasture.
   Uncle Carl has gray ——.
3. A strong breeze blew the door open.
   Anna has a dark —— dress.
4. The sun was shining brightly.
   Isaac was Abraham's ——.

B. Some words in our language have the same or nearly the same meaning. On your paper write the two words from each of the following sets which mean nearly the same.

1. cheerful—sad—glad
2. small—tiny—call
3. find—enjoy—like
4. push—draw—shove

C. Each of the words in the list below tells how something or someone can move. Next to each number on your paper, write the word which best completes that sentence.

slithered   scurried   strutted   limped
galloped   crawled   waddled   tiptoed

1. Uncle John —— painfully on his hurt foot.
2. The mouse —— into its hole.
3. Baby Lois —— out of her crib.
4. Mother —— quietly down the stairs.
5. The ponies —— in the field.
6. A snake —— between the rocks.
7. The ducks —— to the pond.
8. The rooster —— in the barnyard.

D. Some words in our language have opposite meanings. Match each word below with its opposite. Write the correct number and letter together on your paper.

1. hot   6. young   a. holy   f. big
2. day   7. small   b. go   g. late
3. stop   8. huge   c. always   h. bad
4. early   9. good   d. little   i. night
5. never   10. sinful   e. cold   j. old

Pronunciation Key

a	add, can	oi	boy, oil
ā	able, ate	ou	out, cow
â	care, air	o͞o	cool, food
ä	father	o͝o	wood, could
b	bat, cab	p	pen, nap
ch	choose, itch	r	run, hour
d	dog, had	s	stop, hiss
e	met, bend	sh	shoe, ash
ē	see, eat	t	ten, cat
		th	thin, both
f	for, calf	th	these, mother
g	go, dog		
h	hope	u	up, come
		û(r)	earn, burn
i	in, pit	yo͞o	use, few
ī	nice, kind		
		v	vase, even
j	joy, edge	w	won, away
k	cap, look	y	your, you
l	late, cool	z	zoo, raise
m	meet, home	zh	pleasure
n	neat, pin		
ng	sing, wrong	ə	a in comma
			e in oven
o	hot, pod		i in notify
ō	toe, own		o in melon
ô	jaw, order		u in Nahum

Dictionary

Aa

accurate (ak′yər•it) Exact and to the point; without mistake.

ache (āk) To have pain; to be painful; hurt.

action (ak′shən) Movement; that which is done.

adjective (aj′ik•tiv) A word which is used to tell more about a noun and can fit into the blanks in these two sentences:
The —— thing was here.
It is very ——.

aid (ād) Give assistance; help.

alms (ämz) A gift or gifts for the poor.

alphabet (al′fə•bet) The letters used for writing a specific language.

ENGLISH	HEBREW	RUSSIAN
A a	א	A a
B b	בּ , ב	Б б
C c	גּ , ג	Г г

alphabetical order (al′fə•bet′i•kəl ôr′dər) A system in which words are arranged according to the order in which their first letters come in the alphabet.

always (ôl′wāz) At all times; forever.

asleep (ə•slēp′) In a state of sleep; not awake.

astray (ə•strā′) Away from the right path; lost.

aught (ôt) Anything.

awake (ə•wāk′) To bring or come out of sleep.

away (ə•wā′) Not here; gone; out of hearing or out of sight.

Bb

bad (bad) Not good; wicked; evil.

balk (bôk) To be stubborn; refuse to move forward.

be (bē) Exist.

bee (bē) An insect which eats the nectar of flowers; an insect which makes honey.

big (big) Of great size; large.

black (blak) The opposite of white; the color of coal or pitch.

blind (blīnd) Not able to see.

blizzard (bliz′ərd) A severe snowstorm, usually with strong winds.

boy (boi) A man child; a lad.

Braille (brāl) A way of writing for the blind in which each letter of the alphabet is shown by raised dots which can be felt with the fingertips.

brethren (breth′rən) Brothers; members of a church.

burro (bûr′ō) A small donkey.

buzz (buz) A humming sound, as that made by various insects.

Cc

cackle (kak′əl) A short broken sound, like that sometimes made by a hen; a short, shrill laugh.

careless (kâr′lis) Not paying enough attention to what one does; not careful.

chatter (chat′ər) To make short, quick, unclear sounds as do certain birds, monkeys, etc.

cheerful (chir′fəl) Full of cheer; glad; joyful.

chirp (chûrp) The short cry made by a small bird.

chuckle (chuk′əl) To laugh quietly.

clean (klēn) Free from dirt.

cold (kōld) Having little or no heat; the opposite of hot; chilly.

combine (kəm•bīn′) To join together; unite.

comma (kom′ə) The mark (,) used to separate words or phrases.

common noun (kom′ən noun) A noun which does not name a specific person, place, or thing.

complete (kəm•plēt′) Finish; do totally.

conceal (kən•sēl′) Hide; put out of sight.

countenance (koun′tə•nəns) The expression on someone's face.

courteous (kûr′tē•əs) Showing courtesy and good manners; polite.

courtesy (kûr′tə•sē) Good manners; politeness.

crawl (krôl) To move about on the hands and knees; to move slowly with the body close to the ground.

cruel (krōō′əl) Enjoying making or watching people or animals suffer; not kind.

cry (krī) To make a loud sound with the voice; to show sorrow, pain, etc. by sobbing or shedding tears.

cubit (kyōō′bit) A length of eighteen inches; the distance from the elbow to the tip of the fingers.

Dd

day (dā) The time of light between sunrise and sunset.

dead (ded) Without life; no longer living.

deaf (def) Not able to hear.

dear (dir) Precious; very much loved.

deer (dir) A large animal which is found wild in the woods. A baby deer is called a fawn.

definition (def′ə•nish′ən) The meaning of a word.

describe (di•skrīb′) To tell about something or someone; especially to tell how something looks, sounds, feels, tastes, or smells.

dessert (di•zûrt′) The nuts, fruits, or sweet foods which are served at the end of a meal.

dictionary (dik′shən•er′ē) A book which lists words alphabetically and gives each word's correct spelling, pronunciation, and meaning.

disciple (di•sī′pəl) Someone who follows and listens to a teacher; one of the twelve men chosen by Jesus to be His companions when He lived here on earth.

dirty (dûr′tē) Soiled; not clean.

doze (dōz) To sleep lightly; nap.

draw (drô) To make a picture with pen or pencil.

dress (dres) A piece of clothing worn by women or girls, which has a skirt and blouse joined together.

drink (dringk) That which is swallowed to satisfy one's thirst.

dry (drī) Not wet or damp; without moisture.

duck (duk) A bird with webbed feet and a broad bill, and which spends most of its time in the water.

dull (dul) Not sharp, when talking about a knife; not bright, when talking about a color.

Ee

ear (ir) That part of a person or animal which is used for hearing.

early (ûr′lē) Ahead of time; the opposite of late.

easy (ē′zē) Without difficulty; simple; not hard.

empty (emp′tē) Having nothing or no one in it.

enjoy (in•joi′) To take pleasure in doing; like.

enough (i•nuf′) As much as is needed; sufficient.

Ff

famine (fam′in) A lack of enough food for a large area or a large group of people.

find (fīnd) To get or see by searching; to get back something that has been lost.

finish (fin′ish) To complete; to come to the end.

flea (flē) A tiny, blackish brown insect which sucks blood from animals.

flee (flē) To run away quickly; to try to escape.

flock (flok) A group of animals; especially a group of sheep or birds.

frighten (frīt′n) To make afraid; scare.

frown (froun) To wrinkle the forehead and draw the eyebrows together in anger, worry, or deep thought.

Gg

gallop (gal′əp) The fastest that a horse moves.

gentle (jen′təl) Kind and tender.

genuine (jen′yo͞o•in) Real; not pretend.

girl (gûrl) A female child.

glad (glad) Feeling or showing joy; happy.

glance (glans) To look at quickly.

go (gō) To move away; leave; depart.

good (good) As it ought to be; that does what is right; well-behaved.

gravel (grav'əl) A mixture of small stones and bits of rock.

grievous (grē'vəs) Causing sorrow or grief.

grin (grin) A broad smile which shows the teeth.

gruff (gruf) Rough or harsh in speech.

Hh

hair (hâr) The fine, threadlike growths found on a person's or animal's head and skin.

happy (hap'ē) Feeling or showing pleasure or joy; glad.

hard (härd) Difficult, not easy; also, not soft.

hare (hâr) A rabbit-like animal which has long hind legs.

hart (härt) A specific kind of deer.

healthy (hel'thē) Having good health; well.

hear (hir) To listen to; to notice sound.

here (hir) At this place; opposite of *there*.

hike (hīk) To take a long walk, as over a hill, through the woods, or across a field.

hit (hit) To strike.

hobble (hob'əl) To walk slowly with a limp.

holy (hō'lē) Free from sin; pure.

honor (on'ər) Respect.

hop (hop) To spring from the ground on one foot.

hot (hot) Very warm; having a high temperature.

howl (houl) The loud cry made by a wolf or similar animal.

huge (hyo͞oj) Very large.

humble (hum′bəl) Without pride; modest; not boasting of oneself.

hurricane (hûr′ə•kān) A heavy rainstorm with strong, swirling winds.

Ii

impotent (im′pə•tənt) Without power or strength; weak.

in (in) The opposite of *out*.

incarnate (in•kär′nit) Having a bodily form.

indent (in•dent′) To set in from the edge, as with the first line of a paragraph.

index (in′deks) An alphabetical list at the end of a book which lists the songs, names, words, or topics found in that book.

indigo (in′də•gō) A deep violet blue.

inn (in) A place where people who are travelling may stop to eat or sleep.

Jj

jump (jump) To spring from the ground with both feet; leap.

Kk

knew (no͞o) past form of *know*.

knock (nok) To strike or hit; to rap, as at a door.

know (nō) To be sure of or have the facts about.

Ll

lame (lām) Not able to walk properly because of crippled legs or feet.

language (lang′gwij) The ability which God has given to people to use words to speak and to express ideas; the words used by the people of a specific group or country, such as German, English, Spanish, or Hebrew.

large (lärj) Of great size or amount; big.

late (lāt) After the time expected; tardy.

laugh (laf) To make a series of quick sounds with the voice that show one is amused or happy.

letter (let′ər) One of the symbols in an alphabet.

limp (limp) To walk in an uneven way because of a lame leg.

little (lit′l) Small in size; not large.

look (lŏŏk) To turn or aim one's eyes in order to see.

loose (lōōs) Not tight; not attached to anything.

lose (lōōz) To not win, as in a game; to forget where something is, such as *to lose a cap*.

Mm

march (märch) To walk steadily, especially with a group of people.

meat (mēt) Animal flesh which is used for food.

meek (mēk) Gentle; humble, submissive.

meet (mēt) To learn to know someone; to come together at a certain place.

mend (mend) To put back in good condition; repair; fix.

Nn

nap (nap) A short sleep.

narrow (nar′ō) Small in width.

neat (nēt) Orderly; tidy; not sloppy.

neigh (nā) The sound made by a horse.

never (nev'ər) At no time; not ever.

new (no͞o) Seen, made, thought, etc. for the first time.

night (nīt) The time of darkness between sunset and sunrise.

noun (noun) A word which names a person, place, or thing.

nudge (nuj) To push gently.

<u>Oo</u>

old (ōld) Having lived for a long time or been made a long time ago; not new.

omnipotent (om•nip'ə•tənt) Having all power; almighty.

on (on) Attached to; resting upon.

one (wun) Being singular in number.

open (ō'pən) Not closed or shut.

opposite (op'ə•zit) That which is at the other end; that which is the reverse.

oral (ôr'əl) Spoken by the mouth.

order (ôr'dər) An exact way of doing things; a neat, systematic way of doing things.

out (out) Away from the inside.

<u>Pp</u>

pair (pâr) Two people or two things which are related.

paragraph (par'ə•graf) A group of sentences which work together to tell about one subject; a group of sentences in which the first sentence is indented.

parentheses (pə•ren'thə•sēz) The two curved lines ( ) which are used to set apart a word or group of words.

past (past) Having already happened; that time which came before now.

pasture (pas'chər) Land where animals are taken to allow them to eat the grass and other plants which grow there.

pear (pâr) A juicy fruit which has a skin similar to that of an apple, and is usually round like a ball at one end and more pointed at the other end.

peep (pēp) The high-pitched sound made by a small bird or baby chick.

period (pir'ē•əd) A mark used at the end of a telling sentence.

phrase (frāz) A group of words which work together but do not express a complete thought.

play (plā) To have fun; to take part in a game.

plural (plo͝or'əl) Referring to more than one person or thing.

poem (pō'əm) A writing which is done in lines and verse, instead of in paragraph form, and which often has rhyme and rhythm.

polite (pə līt') Showing good manners; being respectful and considerate of others.

potent (pōt'nt) Powerful; describing a medicine which is strong and effective.

prefer (pri•fûr') To like better; to think more highly of one than another.

present (prez'ənt) That which is now; not past or future.

press (pres) To push upon; to apply pressure to.

pronoun (prō'noun) A word that may be used to take the place of a noun or noun phrase.

pronunciation (prə•nun'sē•ā'shən) The way in which a word is said or pronounced.

proper noun (prop′ər noun) A noun that names a specific person, place, or thing and always begins with a capital letter.

proud (proud) Showing pride; thinking too much of oneself.

punctuation (pungk′chōō•ā′shən) The marks, other than the alphabet, which are used when writing, especially those marks which are used to separate series of words or sentences.

? ! ; :

. , ( )

purr (pûr) The soft rumbling sound made by a cat.

, " "

push (pŏŏsh) To press against so as to move; shove.

Qq

question (kwes′chən) A sentence which asks.

question mark (kwes′chən märk) The mark (?) used at the end of a sentence which asks.

Rr

raiment (rā′mənt) Clothing.

ran (ran) The past form of *run*.

rectangular (rek•tang′gyə•lər) Shaped like a rectangle.

respect (ri•spekt′) To esteem; to show honor to.

rhyme (rīm) To match words which have the same end sound.

ripe (rīp) Mature, ready to eat; said of a fruit or vegetable which is not green or immature.

road (rōd) A wide path on which people may travel by foot, car, truck, or the use of animals.

roar (rôr) A deep, rumbling sound, as that made by a lion.

rod (rod) A thin, straight piece of wood, metal, or other material.

rode (rōd) Did ride.

roll book (rōl book) A book in which a teacher may write the names of the class members.

rough (ruf) Coarse; not smooth.

run (run) To move quickly by foot.

Ss

sad (sad) Feeling unhappy.

safe (sāf) Free from danger; secure.

sail (sāl) The piece of fabric which is attached to a boat or ship and is used to catch the wind and help the boat move forward.

sale (sāl) When things are sold.

sandstorm (sand'stôrm') A wind storm which carries dust and sand.

scare (skâr) Frighten; make afraid.

scarlet (skär'lit) A bright red.

scour (skour) To clean by washing with a rough soap or cloth.

scrub (skrub) To wash by rubbing hard.

scurry (skûr'ē) To move quickly but with short steps.

sea (sē) A large body of salt water.

see (sē) To have or use the sense of sight.

seek (sēk) Search; look for; try to find.

sentence (sen'təns) A group of words containing a verb and expressing a complete thought.

shepherd (shep'ərd) A person who takes care of sheep.

short (shôrt) Not measuring much from beginning to end; not long.

shout (shout) A loud, sudden cry or call.

shove (shuv) To push with force.

shrill (shril) A high, sharp sound.

shy (shī) Easily frightened; not comfortable meeting strangers; timid.

sick (sik) Not healthy or well; ill.

sinful (sin′fəl) Full of sin; wicked.

singular (sing′gyə•lər) Referring to only one person or thing.

sip (sip) A small amount of drink swallowed at a time.

sketch (skech) A quickly done drawing which is usually only a simple outline without any details.

sleep (slēp) Slumber; to not be awake.

slither (sliŧħ′ər) To slide along, as does a snake.

slumber (slum′bər) To sleep quietly.

small (smôl) Little in size; not large.

smile (smīl) To turn the corners of the mouth up in order to show pleasure or happiness.

sober (sō′bər) Serious; having a modest manner.

soft (sôft) Not hard; giving easily under pressure.

some (sum) A certain but not a definite number or amount; not all.

sorrowful (sor′ə•fəl) Sad; unhappy.

span (span) A measure of distance as shown by the distance between the tips of the thumb and the little finger when the fingers are spread out; about nine inches.

specific (spi•sif′ik) Exact; definite.

squawk (skwôk) A shrill, harsh sound, as that made by a frightened chicken; the noise made by a parrot.

squeak (skwēk) A sharp, high-pitched sound; the sound made by a mouse.

stale (stāl) Not fresh; having lost favor or freshness.

stare (stâr) To look at something steadily without moving the eyes.

stature (stach′ər) The height of a person or animal.

stop (stop) To halt or keep from going on; bring or come to an end.

stroll (strōl) To walk without an exact purpose or place in mind.

strut (strut) To walk proudly, with head held high and chest thrust forward; especially the way a rooster walks.

stumble (stum′bəl) To trip when walking.

subject (sub′jikt) That which is being spoken or written about.

sum (sum) The result gotten by adding two or more addends.

supplication (sup′lə•kā′shən) A humble prayer.

Tt

tail (tāl) The flexible part of an animal which hangs or extends from the hind end.

tale (tāl) A story.

talk (tôk) Speech; that which is said.

tall (tôl) Reaching a long way up; high.

tame (tām) Harmless; living in peace with man; not wild.

tear (târ) To pull apart by force; rip.

tight (tīt) Put together firmly or closely; fitting too closely.

tiny (tī′nē) Very small.

tiptoe (tip′tō′) To walk on the tips of one's toes in a quiet or careful way.

towards (tə•wôrdz′) In the direction of; leading to.

trip (trip) To stumble; to lose one's balance by catching one's foot against something.

tumult (tōō′mult) Loud noise; commotion; a noisy disturbance.

Uu

under (un′dər) Below or beneath something; the opposite of above.

Vv

variety (və•rī′ə•tē) Difference; that which is not always the same.

verb (vûrb) A word which can correctly complete at least one of these sentences:

I ——.   He —— it.
He ——.   They —— it.
They ——.

vocabulary (vō•kab′yə•ler′ē) A list of words; all the words which a person knows and uses.

Ww

waddle (wod′l) To walk with small steps; swaying from side to side, as a duck does.

wait (wāt) To remain until something expected happens.

walk (wôk) To move on foot at a normal speed.

wash (wosh) To clean with water or other liquid; often with soap.

weak (wēk) Without strength; feeble; not strong.

week (wēk) A period of time made up of seven days.

weight (wāt) How heavy an object is; how much someone or something weighs.

wet (wet) Covered or soaked with water or some other liquid.

whisper (hwis′pər) To speak or say in a low, soft voice.

white (hwīt) The color of pure snow or milk.

wide (wīd) Great in width; measuring much from side to side.

wild (wīld) Not tame; not controlled by man.

will (wil) To decide or choose. A verb used with other verbs in speaking about the future.

won (wun) Have victory; did not lose, as in a game or race.

wood (wŏŏd) The hard material under the bark of a tree.

would (wŏŏd) The past form of *will.*

Xx

X-ray (eks′rā′) A special picture which is taken of one's bones or inner organs by sending rays through the body.

Yy

yak (yak) A large animal, with very long hair, which is related to the cow and buffalo.

yoke (yōk) A curved piece of wood which is placed over a person's shoulders to help in carrying something; also, a curved piece of wood which is used to join two animals together.

young (yung) Being in an early part of life or growth; not old.

Zz

zebra (zē′brə) An animal with dark stripes which is related to the donkey and a horse, and is found wild in Africa.

zoological (zō′ə•loj′i•kəl) Having to do with animals; *zoological park:* a place where animals are kept for people to see.